THE MAMMOTH BOOK OF MATH ACTIVITIES FOR MINECRAFTERS

SUPER FUN

ADDITION, SUBTRACTION, MULTIPLICATION, DIVISION, AND CODE-BREAKING ACTIVITIES!

Sky Pony Press
New York

Sky Pony Press books may be purchased in bulk at special discounts for sales promotion, corporate gifts, fund-raising, or educational purposes. Special editions can also be created to specifications. For details, contact the Special Sales Department, Sky Pony Press, 307 West 36th Street, 11th Floor, New York, NY 10018 or info@skyhorsepublishing.com.

Sky Pony® is a registered trademark of Skyhorse Publishing, Inc.®, a Delaware corporation.

Minecraft® is a registered trademark of Notch Development AB.

The Minecraft game is copyright © Mojang AB.

Visit our website at www.skyponypress.com.

10 9 8 7 6 5 4 3 2 1

Library of Congress Cataloging-in-Publication Data is available on file.

Cover design by Brian Peterson
Cover illustration by Bill Greenhead and Amanda Brack

Interior art by Amanda Brack and Bill Greenhead
Book design by Kevin Baier
Coding Activities by Jen Funk Weber

Print ISBN: 978-1-5107-7114-7

Printed in China

Portions of this book were previously published in *Math for Minecrafters Adventures in Addition and Subtraction: Grades 1–2 (Volume 2)* (ISBN: 978-1-5107-6621-1), *Math for Minecrafters Adventures in Multiplication and Division: Grades 3–4 (Volume 2)* (ISBN: 978-1-5107-6622-8), *Math Fun for Minecrafters: Grades 1–2* (ISBN: 978-1-5107-3760-0), *Math Fun for Minecrafters: Grades 3–4* (ISBN: 978-1-5107-3761-7), and *Math Codes for Minecrafters* (ISBN: 978-1-5107-4724-1)

TABLE OF CONTENTS

A NOTE TO PARENTS

When you want to reinforce classroom skills at home, it's crucial to have kid-friendly learning materials. This workbook transforms math practice into an irresistible adventure complete with diamond armor, zombie pigmen, ghasts, and skeletons. That means less arguing over homework and more fun overall.

The Mammoth Book of Math Activities for Minecrafters is also fully aligned with National Common Core Standards for 1st, 2nd, 3rd, and 4th grade math. What does that mean, exactly? All of the problems in this book correspond to what your child is expected to learn in school. This eliminates confusion and builds confidence for greater homework-time success!

The primary focus of this workbook is math facts repetition and fluency. With enough supplemental practice, your child will commit the answers to common addition and subtraction problems to memory and level up their math ability.

As the workbook progresses, the math problems become more advanced, then ends with fun code-breaking activities. Encourage your child to progress at his or her own pace. Learning is best when students are challenged, but not frustrated. What's most important is that your Minecrafter is engaged in his or her own learning.

Whether it's the joy of seeing their favorite game characters on every page or the thrill of solving challenging problems just like Steve and Alex, there is something in this workbook to entice even the most reluctant math student.

Happy adventuring!

ADDITION AND SUBTRACTION ACTIVITIES

ADDITION BY GROUPING

Circle the groups of 2. Then count on and write the total. The first one is done for you.

1.  Answer: **5**

2.

Answer: _____

3.

Answer: _____

4.

Answer: _____

5.

Answer: _____

MYSTERY MESSAGE
WITH ADDITION AND SUBTRACTION

Add or subtract. Then use the letters to fill in the blanks below and reveal the answer to Alex's joke.

1. 10 - 2 = _____ C

2. 4 + 3 = _____ F

3. 15 - 10 = _____ I

4. 6 + 4 = _____ R

5. 7 + 7 = _____ E

6. 13 - 9 = _____ T

7. 9 + 3 = _____ N

8. 8 - 5 = _____ M

9. 7 + 8 = _____ A

Q: What word could also mean "digging up art"?

Copy the letters from the answers above to solve the joke.

_____ _____ _____ _____ _____ _____ _____ _____ _____
  3   5   12   14   8   10   15   7   4

ADDITION IN BASE 10

Add the numbers.

1. 2 + 3 = _____

2. 4 + 1 = _____

3. 3 + 4 = _____

4. 0 + 5 = _____

5. 7 + 1 = _____

6. 5 + 2 = _____

7. 1 + 6 = _____

8. 4 + 4 = _____

9. 9 + 1 = _____

10. 6 + 4 = _____

SKIP COUNT CHALLENGE

Count by 2s and fill in the empty spaces to help Alex tame her pig.

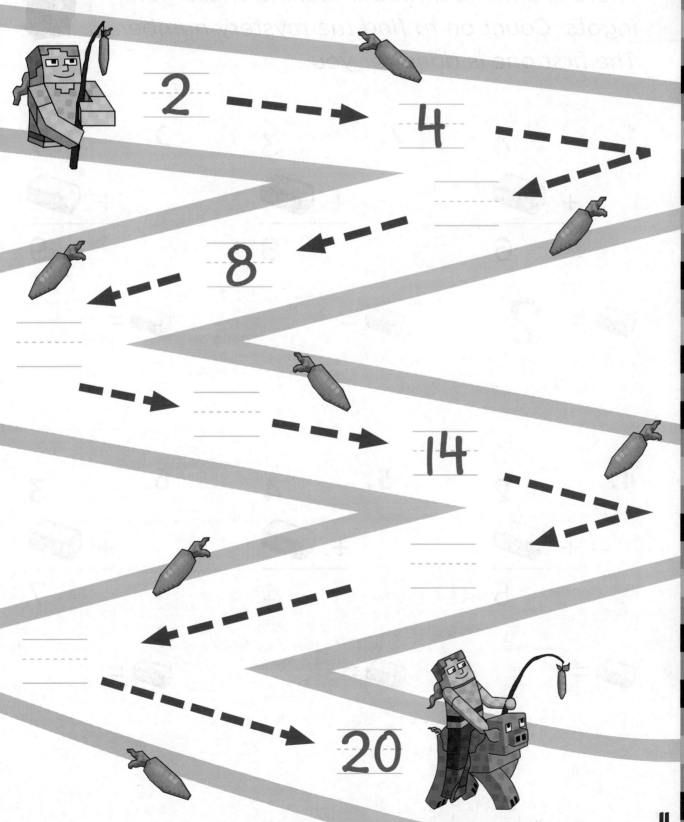

ADDITION MYSTERY NUMBER

There is a number hidden behind these gold ingots. Count on to find the mystery number. The first one is done for you.

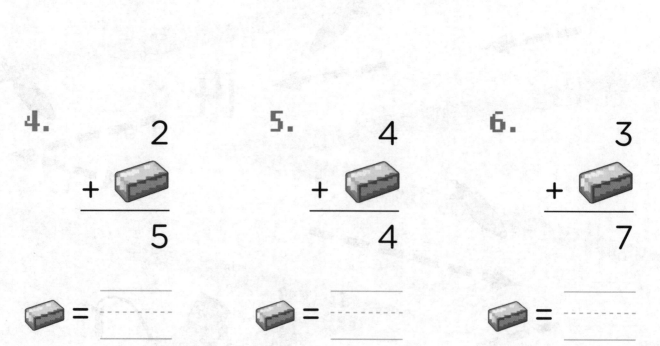

1.
$$\begin{array}{r} 4 \\ + \\ \hline 6 \end{array}$$
= **2**

2.
$$\begin{array}{r} 3 \\ + \\ \hline 8 \end{array}$$
= _____

3.
$$\begin{array}{r} 7 \\ + \\ \hline 9 \end{array}$$
= _____

4.
$$\begin{array}{r} 2 \\ + \\ \hline 5 \end{array}$$
= _____

5.
$$\begin{array}{r} 4 \\ + \\ \hline 4 \end{array}$$
= _____

6.
$$\begin{array}{r} 3 \\ + \\ \hline 7 \end{array}$$
= _____

SUBTRACTION MYSTERY NUMBER

There is a number hidden behind these glowstone blocks. Subtract to find the mystery number. The first one is done for you.

1.
8
- 🔲
___
6

🔲 = **2**

2.
7
- 🔲
___
4

🔲 = _____

3.
2
- 🔲
___
0

🔲 = _____

4.
8
- 🔲
___
5

🔲 = _____

5.
5
- 🔲
___
1

🔲 = _____

6.
9
- 🔲
___
8

🔲 = _____

ADDITION IN BASE 10

Add the numbers. Then write the answer using tally marks. The first one is done for you.

1. 2 + 2 =   4   **TALLY** ||||

2. 3 + 4 =   _____   **TALLY**

3. 1 + 5 =   _____   **TALLY**

4. 3 + 2 =   _____   **TALLY**

5. 2 + 1 =   _____   **TALLY**

6. 4 + 4 =   _____   **TALLY**

SUBTRACTION IN BASE 10

Subtract the numbers. Then write the answer using tally marks. The first one is done for you.

1. 6 - 3 = 3

> **TALLY**
> |||

2. 5 - 1 =

> **TALLY**

3. 7 - 2 =

> **TALLY**

4. 6 - 5 =

> **TALLY**

5. 9 - 3 =

> **TALLY**

6. 10 - 3 =

> **TALLY**

ADDITION BY GROUPING

Circle the groups of 3. Then count on and write the total. The first one is done for you.

1.

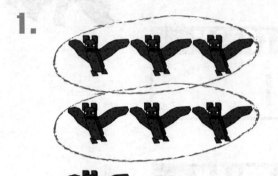

Answer: 7

2.

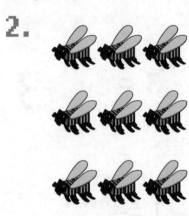

Answer: _____

3.

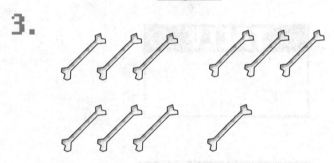

Answer: _____

4.

Answer: _____

5.

Answer: _____

6.

Answer: _____

MYSTERY MESSAGE
WITH ADDITION AND SUBTRACTION

Add or subtract. Then use the letters to fill in the blanks below and reveal the answer to Alex's joke.

1. 7 - 2 = _____ S   2. 4 + 3 = _____ E

3. 9 - 6 = _____ N   4. 6 + 3 = _____ T

5. 8 + 0 = _____ L   6. 9 - 8 = _____ O

7. 9 - 3 = _____ K   8. 10 - 8 = _____ A

Q: What has bones, but not flesh, and a face but no skin?

Copy the letters from the answers above to solve the riddle.

_____ _____ _____ _____ _____ _____ _____ _____ _____

 2   5   6   7   8   7   9   1   3

PUFFER FISH'S GUIDE TO PLACE VALUE

Identify the number that belongs in the place-value chart and write it there. The first one is done for you.

1.

52

TENS
5

2.

73

ONES

3.

25

ONES

4.

62

TENS

5.

21

ONES

6.

30

ONES

7.

42

TENS

8.

94

TENS

SKIP COUNT CHALLENGE

Count by 3s and fill in the empty spaces to help Alex build a giant beacon pyramid.

3

12

21

30

ADDITION AND SUBTRACTION MYSTERY NUMBER

There is a number hidden behind these cobblestone blocks. Add or subtract to find the mystery number. The first one is done for you.

1.

$$7 + \blacksquare = 10$$

$\blacksquare = 3$

2.

$$8 - \blacksquare = 2$$

$\blacksquare =$ ___

3.

$$5 + \blacksquare = 10$$

$\blacksquare =$ ___

4.

$$9 - \blacksquare = 9$$

$\blacksquare =$ ___

5.

$$4 + \blacksquare = 8$$

$\blacksquare =$ ___

6.

$$2 + \blacksquare = 9$$

$\blacksquare =$ ___

7.

$$8 - \blacksquare = 0$$

$\blacksquare =$ ___

8.

$$3 + \blacksquare = 9$$

$\blacksquare =$ ___

MYSTERY MESSAGE

Use the chart to solve the riddle.

3	E
4	R
5	S
6	M
7	O
9	T
10	G
11	N

Q: What's green and black and spawns all over?

___ ___ ___ ___ ___ ___ ___
6 7 11 5 9 3 4

___ ___ ___
3 10 10

ADDITION IN BASE 10

Add the numbers.

1. 2 + 8 = _____

2. 4 + 6 = _____

3. 3 + 7 = _____

4. 5 + 5 = _____

5. 7 + 3 = _____

6. 6 + 4 = _____

7. 9 + 1 = _____

8. 4 + 6 = _____

9. 1 + 9 = _____

10. 8 + 2 = _____

SUBTRACTION IN BASE 10

Subtract the numbers.

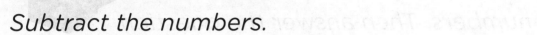

1. 10 - 8 = _____

2. 10 - 6 = _____

3. 10 - 7 = _____

4. 10 - 5 = _____

5. 10 - 3 = _____

6. 10 - 4 = _____

7. 10 - 1 = _____

8. 10 - 0 = _____

9. 10 - 9 = _____

10. 10 - 2 = _____

ADDITION MATH FACTS WITH 0 AND 1

Add the numbers. Then answer the question.

1. $1 + 0 =$

2. $1 + 1 =$

3. $2 + 0 =$

4. $2 + 1 =$

5. $3 + 0 =$

6. $3 + 1 =$

7. $4 + 0 =$

8. $4 + 1 =$

9. $5 + 0 =$

10. $5 + 1 =$

11. $6 + 0 =$

12. $6 + 1 =$

13. $7 + 0 =$

14. $7 + 1 =$

15. $8 + 0 =$

16. $8 + 1 =$

17. $9 + 0 =$

18. $9 + 1 =$

19. $10 + 0 =$

20. $10 + 1 =$

ADDITION MATH FACTS WITH 2 AND 3

Add the numbers.

1. $1 + 2 =$ _____

2. $1 + 3 =$ _____

3. $2 + 2 =$ _____

4. $2 + 3 =$ _____

5. $3 + 2 =$ _____

6. $3 + 3 =$ _____

7. $4 + 2 =$ _____

8. $4 + 3 =$ _____

9. $5 + 2 =$ _____

10. $5 + 3 =$ _____

11. $6 + 2 =$ _____

12. $6 + 3 =$ _____

13. $7 + 2 =$ _____

14. $7 + 3 =$ _____

15. $8 + 2 =$ _____

16. $3 + 6 =$ _____

17. $5 + 2 =$ _____

18. $4 + 3 =$ _____

19. $0 + 2 =$ _____

20. $0 + 3 =$ _____

SKELETON'S GUIDE TO PLACE VALUE

Use the number on each skeleton to fill in the place-value chart.

Example:

Tens	Ones
3	2

1.

Tens	Ones

2.

Tens	Ones

3.

Tens	Ones

4.

Tens	Ones

5.

Tens	Ones

6.

Tens	Ones

SKIP COUNT CHALLENGE

Count by 4s and fill in the empty spaces to help Steve craft his diamond armor.

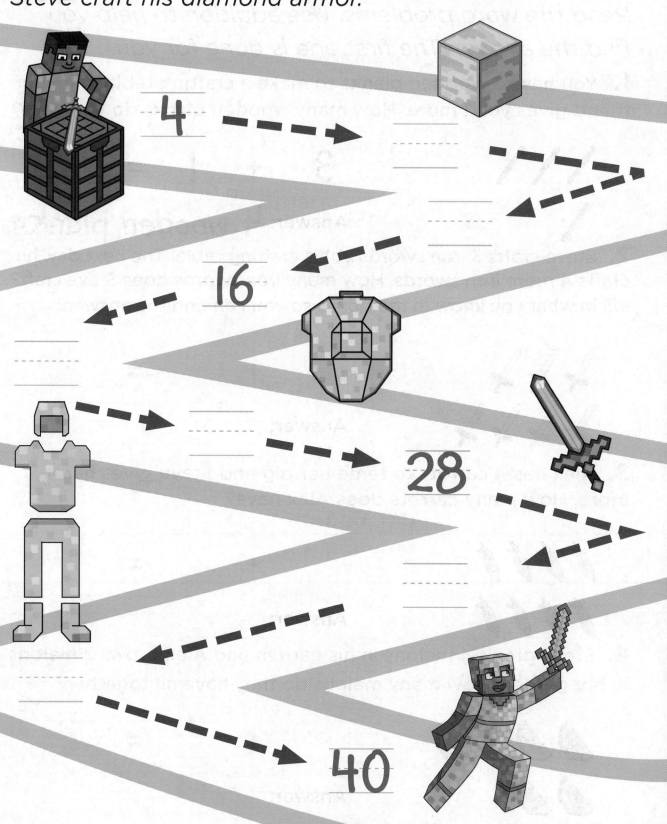

4

16

28

40

WORD PROBLEMS WITH ADDITION

Read the word problems. Use addition to help you find the answer. The first one is done for you.

1. You have 3 wooden planks to make a crafting table and your friend gives you 1 more. How many wooden planks do you have?

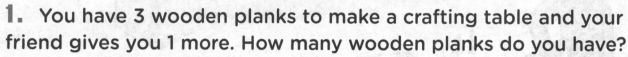

$$3 + 1 = 4$$

Answer: 4 wooden planks

2. Steve crafts 3 iron swords at his crafting table. The next day, he crafts 4 more iron swords. How many iron swords does Steve craft? Fill in what you know in the boxes so you can find the answer.

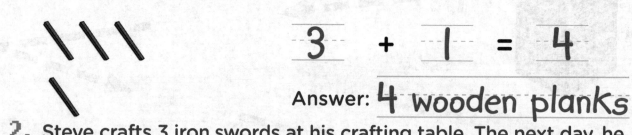

_____ + _____ = _____

Answer: _____

3. Alex has 4 carrots to tame her pig and Steve gives her 4 more. How many carrots does Alex have?

_____ + _____ = _____

Answer: _____

4. Steve grows 4 melons in his garden and Alex grows 2 melons in her garden. How many melons do they have all together?

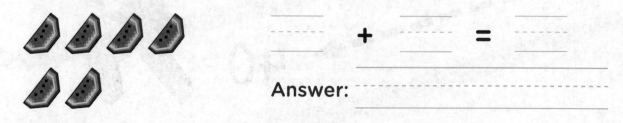

_____ + _____ = _____

Answer: _____

WORD PROBLEMS WITH SUBTRACTION

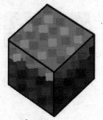

Read the word problems. Use subtraction to help you find the answer. The first one is done for you.

1. You have 8 diamond blocks and use 3 to craft a helmet. How many diamond blocks do you have left?

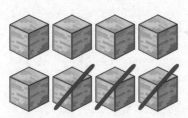

$$8 - 3 = 5$$

Answer: 5 diamond blocks

2. Alex has 10 TNT blocks. She uses 5 TNT blocks to blow up a mob's hiding place. How many blocks does she have left?

_____ - _____ = _____

Answer: _____

3. Steve adds 5 shulker spawn eggs to his inventory. Later that day, he uses 3 of them. How many shulker spawn eggs are in his inventory?

_____ - _____ = _____

Answer: _____

4. Alex crafts 8 wooden swords in the morning. In the afternoon, she breaks 3 of them fighting zombies. How many wooden swords does Alex have left?

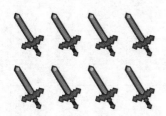

_____ - _____ = _____

Answer: _____

ADDITION IN BASE 10

Add the numbers. Then answer the questions.

1. 4 + 2 = _____

2. 2 + 5 = _____

3. 6 + 3 = _____

4. 4 + 1 = _____

5. 8 + 1 = _____

6. 4 + 6 = _____

7. 2 + 5 = _____

8. 6 + 2 = _____

Q: Circle the answers that are even. What do you notice when you add an even number to an even number?

A: _____

Q: Circle the answers that are odd. What do you notice when you add an even number to an odd number?

A: _____

ADDITION IN BASE 10

Add the numbers. Then answer the questions.

1. 8 - 2 =

2. 10 - 6 =

3. 9 - 2 =

4. 7 - 4 =

5. 8 - 4 =

6. 7 - 6 =

7. 9 - 4 =

8. 10 - 8 =

Q: Circle the answers that are even. What do you notice when you subtract an even number from an even number?

A:

Q: Circle the answers that are odd. What do you notice when you subtract an even number from an odd number?

A:

ADDITION MATH FACTS WITH 4 AND 5

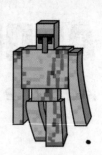

Add the numbers.

1. 1 + 4 = _____

2. 1 + 5 = _____

3. 2 + 4 = _____

4. 2 + 5 = _____

5. 3 + 4 = _____

6. 3 + 5 = _____

7. 4 + 4 = _____

8. 4 + 5 = _____

9. 5 + 4 = _____

10. 5 + 5 = _____

11. 6 + 4 = _____

12. 6 + 5 = _____

13. 7 + 4 = _____

14. 7 + 5 = _____

15. 8 + 4 = _____

16. 8 + 5 = _____

17. 9 + 4 = _____

18. 9 + 5 = _____

19. 10 + 4 = _____

20. 10 + 5 = _____

PROPERTIES OF ADDITION

A sneaky witch swapped the order of the numbers in the equations below. Switch the numbers back and solve both equations.

Example: $1 + 2 = \underline{3}$

$2 + 1 = 3$

1. $3 + 4 = \underline{\qquad}$

2. $5 + 3 = \underline{\qquad}$

3. $7 + 2 = \underline{\qquad}$

4. $8 + 1 = \underline{\qquad}$

5. $4 + 5 = \underline{\qquad}$

6. $10 + 0 = \underline{\qquad}$

What do you notice about the answers in each pair?

MOOSHROOM'S GUIDE TO PLACE VALUE

Identify the number that belongs in the place-value chart and write it there. The first one is done for you.

1.

 392

TENS
9

2.

 874

HUNDREDS

3.

 705

ONES

4.

 304

TENS

5.

 297

HUNDREDS

6.

 430

ONES

7.

 865

TENS

8.

 329

HUNDREDS

SKIP COUNT CHALLENGE

Count by 5s and fill in the empty spaces to help the arctic fox get to the snowy Taiga biome before the wolf catches it.

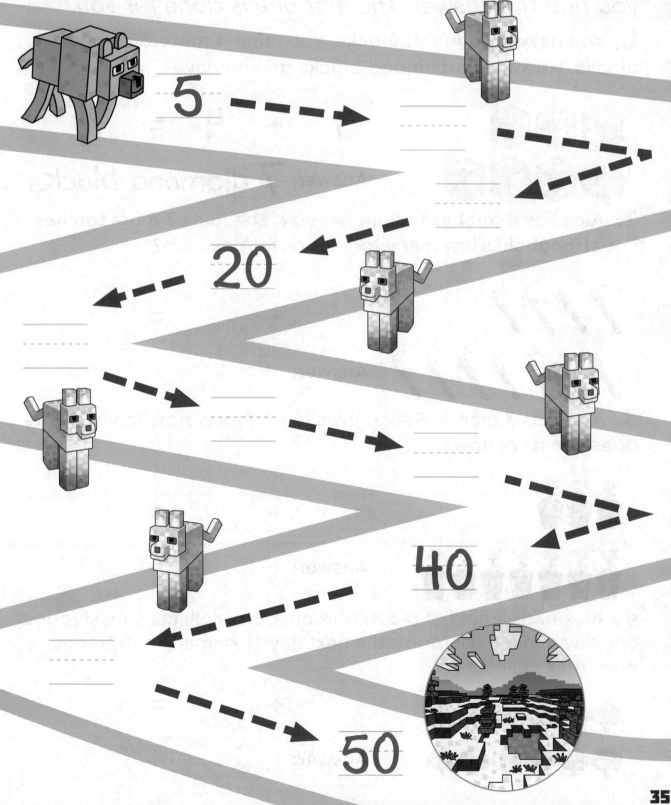

5

20

40

50

WORD PROBLEMS WITH ADDITION

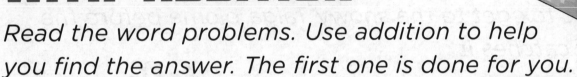

Read the word problems. Use addition to help you find the answer. The first one is done for you.

1. You have 3 diamond blocks. You mine 4 more diamond blocks. How many diamond blocks do you have?

$$3 + 4 = 7$$

Answer: 7 diamond blocks

2. Alex has 4 torches to light her way. She finds 7 more torches in a stronghold. How many torches does Alex have?

___ + ___ = ___

Answer: _____

3. Alex has 3 plants. Steve gives her 7 more. How many plants does she have now?

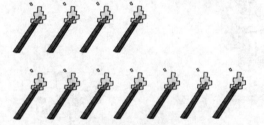

___ + ___ = ___

Answer: _____

4. Alex finds a field of red mushrooms. She collects 6 mushrooms one day and 6 mushrooms the next day. How many mushrooms does Alex collect?

___ + ___ = ___

Answer: _____

WORD PROBLEMS WITH SUBTRACTION

Read the word problems. Use subtraction to help you find the answer. The first one is done for you.

1. There are 9 tools in your inventory. You use 6 of them. How many tools do you have left?

$$9 - 6 = 3$$

Answer: __3 tools__

2. Steve grows 12 sugar cane plants in his garden. He uses 7 of the plants to make paper. How many plants does Steve have left?

_____ - _____ = _____

Answer: _____

3. Alex has 12 horses on her farm. She put saddles on 4 of them. How many horses do not have saddles?

_____ - _____ = _____

Answer: _____

4. Steve crafts 10 pumpkin pies. He eats 3 of them. How many pies are left?

_____ - _____ = _____

Answer: _____

ADDITION AND PLACE VALUE

Add the numbers. Then write the values in the boxes. The first one is done for you.

1. $9 + 6 =$ 15

Tens	Ones
1	5

2. $10 + 2 =$

Tens	Ones

3. $8 + 6 =$

Tens	Ones

4. $17 + 3 =$

Tens	Ones

5. $8 + 5 =$

Tens	Ones

6. $11 + 9 =$

Tens	Ones

SUBTRACTION AND PLACE VALUE

Subtract the numbers. Then write the values in the boxes. The first one is done for you.

1. 20 - 11 =   9

Tens	Ones
0	9

2. 18 - 12 =

Tens	Ones

3. 17 - 7 =

Tens	Ones

4. 11 - 4 =

Tens	Ones

5. 20 - 4 =

Tens	Ones

6. 13 - 13 =

Tens	Ones

SUBTRACTION MATH FACTS FROM 0 TO 10

Subtract the numbers.

1. 10 - 2 = ----------

2. 7 - 3 = ----------

3. 10 - 6 = ----------

4. 6 - 3 = ----------

5. 6 - 6 = ----------

6. 10 - 4 = ----------

7. 8 - 4 = ----------

8. 10 - 3 = ----------

9. 7 - 4 = ----------

10. 5 - 4 = ----------

11. 9 - 4 = ----------

12. 10 - 5 = ----------

13. 3 - 1 = ----------

14. 8 - 3 = ----------

15. 6 - 2 = ----------

16. 7 - 5 = ----------

17. 9 - 2 = ----------

18. 10 - 7 = ----------

19. 6 - 1 = ----------

20. 6 - 4 = ----------

SUBTRACTION MATH FACTS FROM 0 TO 10

Subtract the numbers.

1. 10 - 4 = _____

2. 7 - 4 = _____

3. 8 - 3 = _____

4. 6 - 3 = _____

5. 6 - 5 = _____

6. 9 - 1 = _____

7. 9 - 5 = _____

8. 7 - 5 = _____

9. 10 - 3 = _____

10. 10 - 7 = _____

11. 9 - 6 = _____

12. 9 - 1 = _____

13. 5 - 1 = _____

14. 6 - 4 = _____

15. 8 - 4 = _____

16. 7 - 3 = _____

17. 8 - 2 = _____

18. 10 - 2 = _____

19. 10 - 6 = _____

20. 9 - 4 = _____

LLAMA'S GUIDE TO PLACE VALUE

Use the number on the llama to fill in the place value chart.

Example:

238

Hundreds	
2	
Tens	**Ones**
3	**8**

1.

629

Hundreds	
Tens	**Ones**

2.

708

Hundreds	
Tens	**Ones**

3.

319

Hundreds	
Tens	**Ones**

4.

830

Hundreds	
Tens	**Ones**

5.

985

Hundreds	
Tens	**Ones**

6.

304

Hundreds	
Tens	**Ones**

SKIP COUNT CHALLENGE

Count by 6s and fill in the empty spaces to help Steve escape the zombie.

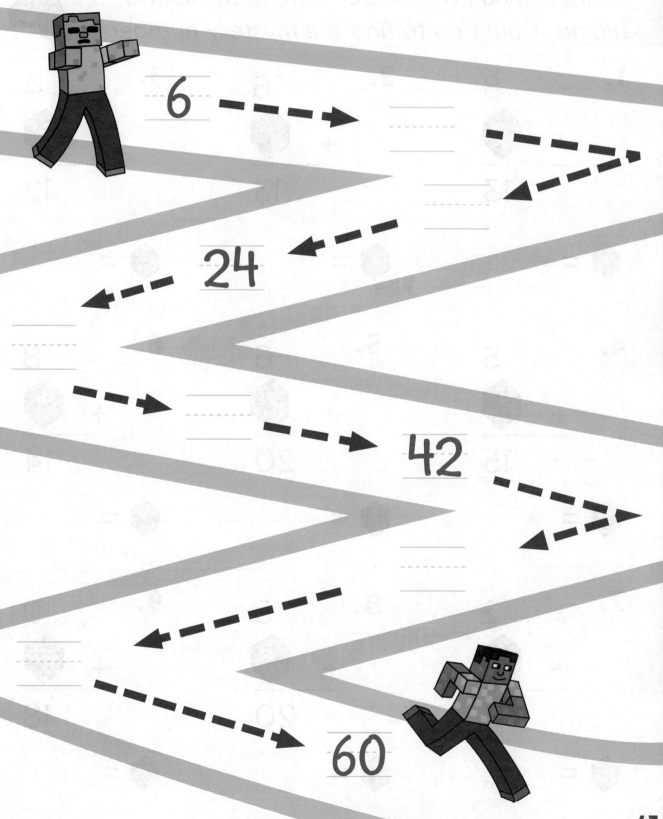

6 ➔ _____

_____ ➔ _____

24 ➔ _____

_____ ➔ _____ ➔ 42 ➔ _____

_____

_____ ➔ 60

ADDITION MYSTERY NUMBER

There is a number hidden behind these lava blocks. Count on to find the mystery number.

1.

$$\begin{array}{r} 8 \\ + \quad \text{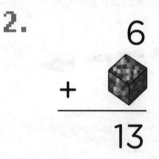} \\ \hline 13 \end{array}$$

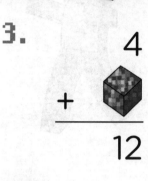 = _____

2.

$$\begin{array}{r} 6 \\ + \\ \hline 13 \end{array}$$

= _____

3.

$$\begin{array}{r} 4 \\ + \\ \hline 12 \end{array}$$

= _____

4.

$$\begin{array}{r} 5 \\ + \\ \hline 15 \end{array}$$

= _____

5.

$$\begin{array}{r} 6 \\ + \\ \hline 20 \end{array}$$

= _____

6.

$$\begin{array}{r} 8 \\ + \\ \hline 14 \end{array}$$

= _____

7.

$$\begin{array}{r} 2 \\ + \\ \hline 8 \end{array}$$

= _____

8.

$$\begin{array}{r} 5 \\ + \\ \hline 20 \end{array}$$

= _____

9.

$$\begin{array}{r} 9 \\ + \\ \hline 18 \end{array}$$

= _____

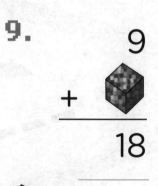

MYSTERY MESSAGE WITH ADDITION

Add the answers from page 40 to the chart.
Then use the chart to solve the riddle.

QUESTION	ANSWER	LETTER
1.		N
2.		B
3.		K
4.		E
5.		Y
6.		I
7.		U
8.		R
9.		L

Q: What's cute and cuddly and fuzzy and deadly?

Copy the letters from the chart to solve the riddle.

8   14   9   9   10   15

7   6   5   5   14

EXPANDED FORM IN BASE 10

Write the number on each polar bear in expanded form in the space provided.

Example:

$$20 + 5$$

1.

2.

3.

4.

5.

6.

EXPANDED FORM IN BASE 10

Write the number on each ocelot in expanded form in the space provided.

Example:

200 + 50 + 6

256

1.

324

_____

2.

849

_____

3.

670

_____

4.

506

_____

5.

932

_____

6.

481

_____

ADDITION BY GROUPING

Circle the groups of 5. Then count on and write the total. The first one is done for you.

1.

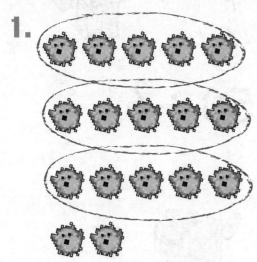

Answer: 17

2.

Answer: _____

3.

Answer: _____

4.

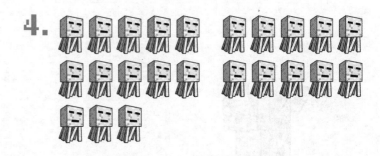

Answer: _____

5.

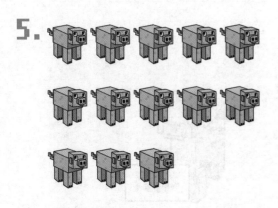

Answer: _____

6.

Answer: _____

MYSTERY MESSAGE
WITH ADDITION AND SUBTRACTION

Add or subtract. Then use the letters to fill in the blanks below and reveal the answer to Steve's joke.

1. 20 - 2 = _____ **S**

2. 14 + 3 = _____ **F**

3. 15 - 9 = _____ **A**

4. 6 + 13 = _____ **R**

5. 7 + 8 = _____ **E**

6. 13 - 6 = _____ **V**

7. 9 + 4 = _____ **L**

8. 18 - 6 = _____ **H**

Q: What do you call a silverfish that doesn't have any eyes?

Copy the letters from the answers above to solve the joke.

_____ _____ _____ _____ _____ _____ _____ _____ _____

6   18   13   7   15   19   17   18   12

SNOW GOLEM'S GUIDE TO PLACE VALUE

Write the number on the snow golem that matches the place value in the chart. The first one is done for you.

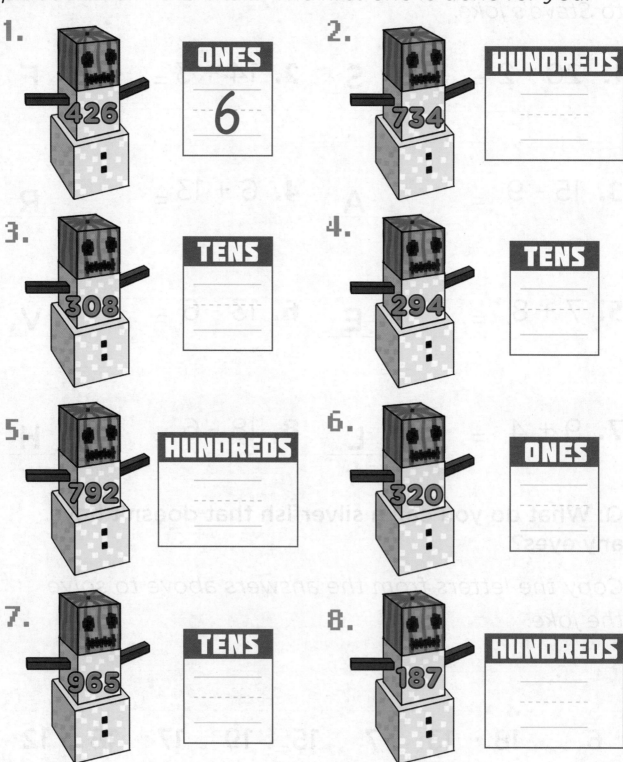

1. 426

ONES
6

2. 734

HUNDREDS

3. 308

TENS

4. 294

TENS

5. 792

HUNDREDS

6. 320

ONES

7. 965

TENS

8. 187

HUNDREDS

SKIP COUNT CHALLENGE

Count by 7s and fill in the empty spaces to help the witch get to the witch's hut.

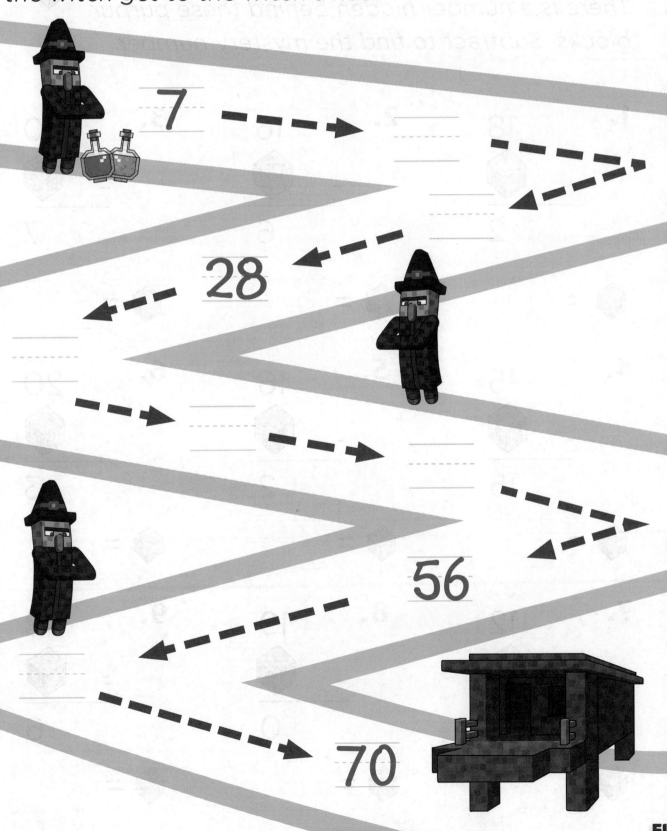

SUBTRACTION MYSTERY NUMBER

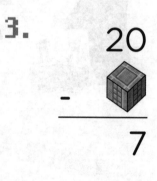

There is a number hidden behind these purpur blocks. Subtract to find the mystery number.

1.

18
-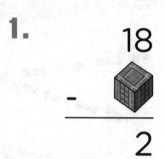
———
2

⬛ = ------------------

2.

16
-
———
6

⬛ = ------------------

3.

20
-
———
7

⬛ = ------------------

4.

15
-
———
15

⬛ = ------------------

5.

16
-
———
2

⬛ = ------------------

6.

20
-
———
3

⬛ = ------------------

7.

12
-
———
1

⬛ = ------------------

8.

19
-
———
0

⬛ = ------------------

9.

18
-
———
6

⬛ = ------------------

MYSTERY MESSAGE WITH SUBTRACTION

Add the answers from page 48 to the chart.
Then use the chart to solve the riddle.

QUESTION	ANSWER	LETTER
1.		N
2.		A
3.		E
4.		T
5.		M
6.		I
7.		R
8.		H
9.		G

Q: What do you call a Minecraft horse wandering after dark?

Copy the letters from the chart to solve the riddle.

____ ____ ____ ____ ____ ____ -
10   16   17   12   19   0

____ ____ ____ ____
14   10   11   13

ADDITION IN BASE 10

Add the numbers. Then draw a line to the box with the correct place value. The first one is done for you.

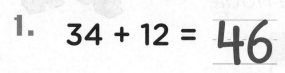

1. 34 + 12 = **46**

2. 17 + 12 = _____

3. 21 + 54 = _____

4. 17 + 71 = _____

5. 25 + 32 = _____

6. 11 + 51 = _____

7. 10 + 4 = _____

8. 31 + 6 = _____

ONES
8

TENS
5

TENS
4

ONES
2

TENS
7

ONES
9

TENS
3

ONES
4

SUBTRACTION IN BASE 10

Subtract the numbers. Then draw a line to the box with the correct place value. The first one is done for you.

1. 36 - 12 = **24**

2. 54 - 24 =

3. 67 - 25 =

4. 73 - 61 =

5. 87 - 21 =

6. 69 - 12 =

7. 99 - 18 =

8. 59 - 20 =

ONES
6

TENS
3

TENS
8

ONES
4

TENS
4

ONES
7

TENS
1

ONES
9

ADDITION MATH FACTS WITH 6 AND 7

Add the numbers.

1. 1 + 6 = ...

2. 1 + 7 = ...

3. 2 + 6 = ...

4. 2 + 7 = ...

5. 3 + 6 = ...

6. 3 + 7 = ...

7. 4 + 6 = ...

8. 4 + 7 = ...

9. 5 + 6 = ...

10. 5 + 7 = ...

11. 6 + 6 = ...

12. 6 + 7 = ...

13. 7 + 6 = ...

14. 7 + 7 = ...

15. 8 + 6 = ...

16. 8 + 7 = ...

17. 9 + 6 = ...

18. 9 + 7 = ...

19. 10 + 6 = ...

20. 10 + 7 = ...

MYSTERY MESSAGE
WITH ADDITION AND SUBTRACTION

Add or subtract. Then use the letters to fill in the blanks below and reveal the answer to Alex's joke.

1. 13 - 2 = _____ M

2. 4 + 16 = _____ A

3. 15 - 7 = _____ S

4. 6 + 13 = _____ R

5. 17 - 7 = _____ W

6. 13 - 8 = _____ I

7. 12 + 3 = _____ O

8. 16 - 9 = _____ D

Q: I'm very sharp and I'm always making a point. What am I?

Copy the letters from the answers above to solve the joke.

_____ _____ _____ _____
5   20   11   20

_____ _____ _____ _____ _____
8   10   15   19   7

ADDITION AND SUBTRACTION MATH FACTS 1–20

Add or subtract to find the answers.

1. $9 + 2 =$

2. $8 + 3 =$

3. $17 - 9 =$

4. $16 - 5 =$

5. $9 + 7 =$

6. $12 - 5 =$

7. $5 + 7 =$

8. $9 + 9 =$

9. $12 - 4 =$

10. $7 + 7 =$

11. $5 + 9 =$

12. $16 - 8 =$

13. $7 + 6 =$

14. $8 + 4 =$

15. $14 - 8 =$

16. $4 + 7 =$

17. $12 - 9 =$

18. $4 + 9 =$

19. $15 - 7 =$

20. $7 + 8 =$

SKIP COUNT CHALLENGE

Count by 8s and fill in the empty spaces to help Alex reach the End portal.

8

32

64

80

WORD PROBLEMS WITH ADDITION

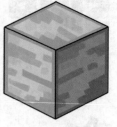

Read the word problems. Use addition to find the answer. The first one is done for you.

1. You mine 3 iron ore blocks, 1 diamond ore block, and 5 granite blocks. How many blocks do you mine in all?

$$3 + 1 + 5 = 9$$

Answer: 9 blocks

2. Alex crafts 2 gold swords at her craft table. The next day, she crafts 4 iron swords. The next day, she crafts 6 diamond swords. How many swords does Alex make?

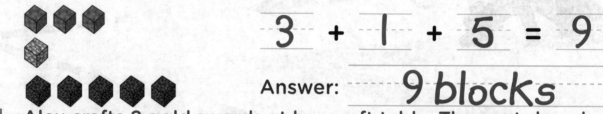

___ + ___ + ___ = ___

Answer: _____

3. In his garden, Steve grows 7 carrots, 2 melons, and 6 potatoes. How many crops does Steve grow?

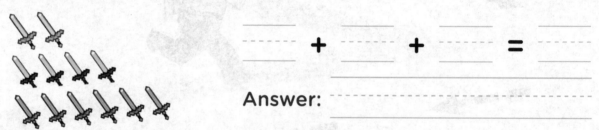

___ + ___ + ___ = ___

Answer: _____

4. Alex battles 5 ghasts, 3 skeletons, and 8 iron golems. How many mobs does Alex battle?

___ + ___ + ___ = ___

Answer: _____

WORD PROBLEMS WITH SUBTRACTION

Read the word problems. Use subtraction to find the answer. The first one is done for you.

1. The librarian has 20 books in the library. Alex borrows 5 books and Steve borrows 3 books. How many books are left?

20 - 5 - 3 = 12

Answer: 12 blocks

2. There are 18 fish in the lake. Steve catches 4 fish one day and 3 fish the next day. How many fish are left in the lake?

_____ - _____ = _____

Answer: _____

3. Alex sees 15 ocelots in the jungle biome. She tames 7 ocelots and Steve tames 5 ocelots. How many untamed ocelots are left?

_____ - _____ = _____

Answer: _____

4. There are 12 skeletons. Alex destroys 2 skeletons and Steve destroys 4 skeletons. How many skeletons are left?

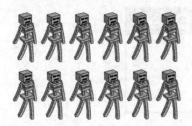

_____ - _____ = _____

Answer: _____

ADDITION AND PLACE VALUE

Add the numbers. Then write the values in the boxes. The first one is done for you.

1. 6 + 7 =   13

Tens	Ones
1	3

2. 8 + 4 =   _____

Tens	Ones

3. 9 + 6 =   _____

Tens	Ones

4. 16 + 4 =   _____

Tens	Ones

5. 8 + 8 =   _____

Tens	Ones

6. 12 + 8 =   _____

Tens	Ones

SUBTRACTION AND PLACE VALUE

Subtract the numbers. Then write the values in the boxes. The first one is done for you.

1. 20 - 13 = 7

Tens	Ones
0	7

2. 17 - 11 =

Tens	Ones

3. 19 - 9 =

Tens	Ones

4. 15 - 10 =

Tens	Ones

5. 20 - 7 =

Tens	Ones

6. 14 - 5 =

Tens	Ones

ADDITION BY GROUPING

Circle groups of 10. Then count and write the numbers.

Example:

1.

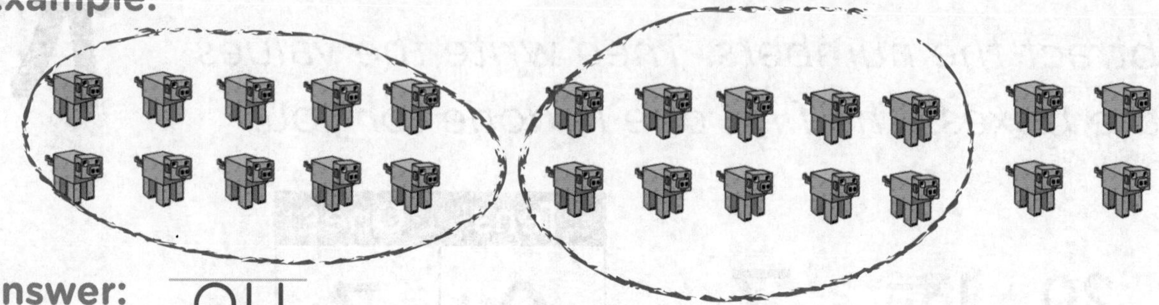

Answer: 24

2.

Answer: _____

3.

Answer: _____

4.

Answer: _____

5.

Answer: _____

MYSTERY MESSAGE
WITH ADDITION
AND SUBTRACTION

Add or subtract. Then use the letters to fill in the blanks below and reveal the answer to Steve's joke.

1. 4 + 8 = 12 F   **5.** 8 – 1 = ___ K

2. 9 – 3 = ___ C   **6.** 9 + 7 = ___ B

3. 6 + 8 = ___ O   **7.** 8 – 3 = ___ L

4. 8 + 3 = ___ A   **8.** 4 + 9 = ___ E

Q: What's the top social network for Minecrafters?

A: _____

COPY THE LETTERS FROM THE ANSWERS ABOVE TO SOLVE THE MYSTERY.

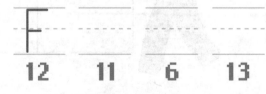

F ___ ___ ___
12   11   6   13

___ ___ ___ ___ ___
16   5   14   6   7

ZOMBIE'S GUIDE TO PLACE VALUE

Use the number on each zombie to fill in the place-value chart. Then, write the number in tally marks.

Example: 1.

Tens	Ones
2	4

‖‖‖ ‖‖‖
‖‖‖ ‖‖‖   ‖‖‖‖

2.

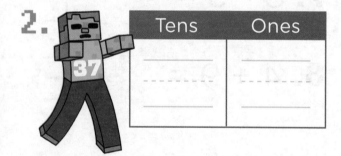

Tens	Ones

3.

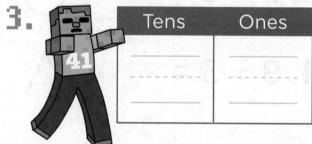

Tens	Ones

4.

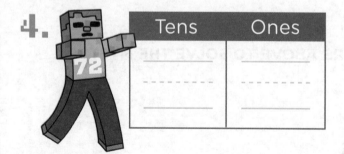

Tens	Ones

5.

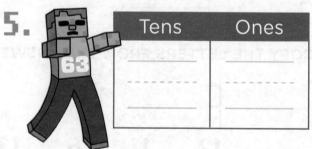

Tens	Ones

6.

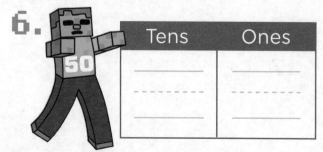

Tens	Ones

7.

Tens	Ones

SKIP COUNT CHALLENGE

Count by 2s and fill in the empty spaces to keep Steve at a safe distance from the blaze.

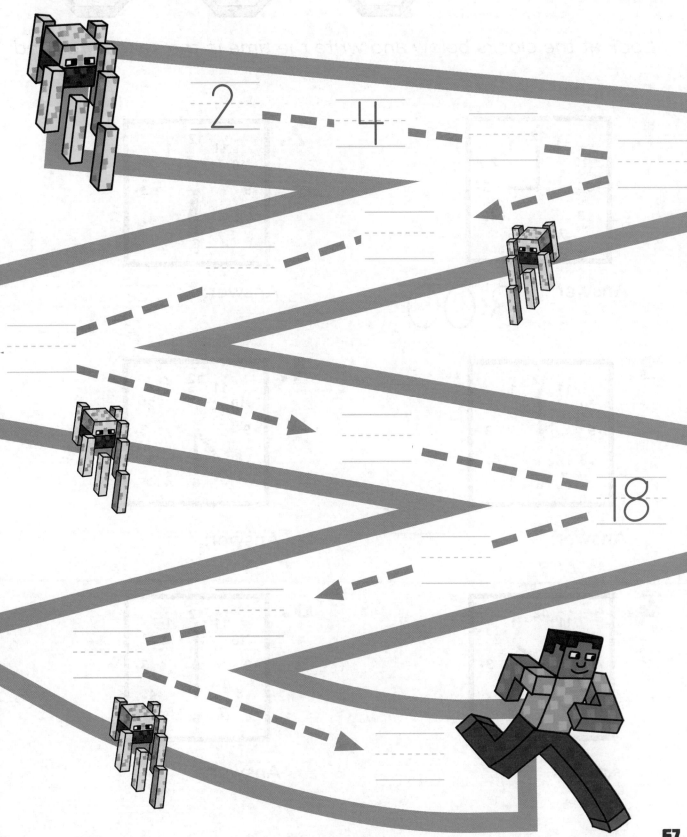

2   4   ___   ___   ___   ___   ___   18   ___   ___   ___

TELLING TIME

 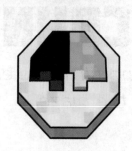 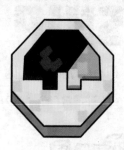

Look at the clocks below and write the time in the space provided:

Example:

1.

Answer:  3:00

2.

Answer: _____

3.

Answer: _____

4.

Answer: _____

5.

Answer: _____

6.

Answer: _____

COUNTING MONEY

The villagers are letting you trade coins for emeralds. Add up your coins to see how much money you have.

25¢   10¢   5¢   1¢

1. 25¢ + 10¢ + 5¢ + 5¢ = **45**¢

2. 10¢ + 5¢ + 5¢ + 1¢ =

3. 25¢ + 5¢ + 1¢ =

4. 25¢ + 10¢ + 5¢ + 1¢ =

5. 10¢ + 10¢ + 5¢ + 5¢ + 1¢ =

6. 25¢ + 5¢ + 5¢ + 5¢ + 1¢ =

7. 25¢ + 10¢ + 10¢ + 1¢ + 1¢ =

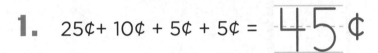

HARDCORE MODE: *Try this hardcore math challenge!*

8. One villager charges 30¢ for each emerald. How many dimes do you need in order to buy an emerald?

Answer:

69

ADVENTURES IN GEOMETRY

Let's learn about fractions! Count the number of squares in the crafting grid below, and write it on the line.

1. Color three of the four squares green

This is called three-fourths, or ¾.

2. Steve breaks this crafting grid into two equal parts. Color one of the two parts yellow.

This is called one half, or ½.

3. Count the rectangles in the experience bar below.
Write the number here: _____

4. This experience bar is divided into 3 equal parts.
Color one part blue.

This is called one third, or ⅓.

5. This experience bar is divided into 3 equal parts.
Color two parts blue.

This is called two thirds, or ⅔.

HARDCORE MODE: *Try this hardcore math challenge!*
This health bar shows 9 hearts. Color in 3 hearts below.

Circle the fraction that describes how many are colored in:

A. 1/2   B. 1/4   C. 1/3

WORD PROBLEMS

Read the problem carefully. Use the picture to help you solve the problem. Fill in your answer.

Example:

You get 8 minutes of daylight in Minecraft. You lose 4 minutes building a shelter and finding food. How many minutes are left?

8 - 4 = 4

Answer: 4 minutes

1. You need 4 wooden planks to make a crafting table, but you only have 2. How many more planks do you need?

Answer: _____

2. There are 7 empty spaces in your inventory bar. You fill 3 spaces with tools. How many empty spaces do you have?

Answer: _____

3. You shear a mooshroom cow and 7 red mushrooms appear. You eat 4 of them. How many mushrooms are left?

Answer: _____

72

4. You have 5 goats on your farm. You add 3 cows to the farm. How many animals do you have?

Answer: _____

5. You have 6 glass blocks. You get 3 more blocks. How many glass blocks do you have?

Answer: _____

6. There are 7 zombies chasing you. Thankfully, 4 of them fall in a lava pit! How many zombies are still chasing you?

Answer: _____

7. Alex has 5 axes in her inventory. She crafts 2 more axes. How many axes does she have?

Answer: _____

8. Yesterday 3 skeletons spawned in the Overworld. Today 6 spawned. How many more skeletons spawned today than yesterday?

Answer: _____

GHAST GUIDE TO PLACE VALUE

Read the number above each ghast to fill in the place-value chart. Then, write the number in tally marks.

Example:

1. **15**

Tens	Ones
1	5

|||| |||| ||||

2. **27**

Tens	Ones

3. **86**

Tens	Ones

4. **32**

Tens	Ones

5. **71**

Tens	Ones

6. **60**

Tens	Ones

7. **54**

Tens	Ones

SKIP COUNT CHALLENGE

The baby zombie is tired after a long night of fighting. Count by 3s and help him find shelter before the sun rises.

ALL IN A DAY'S WORK

A Minecrafter's first day is very busy!
Match the time for each task on the left with a clock on the right.

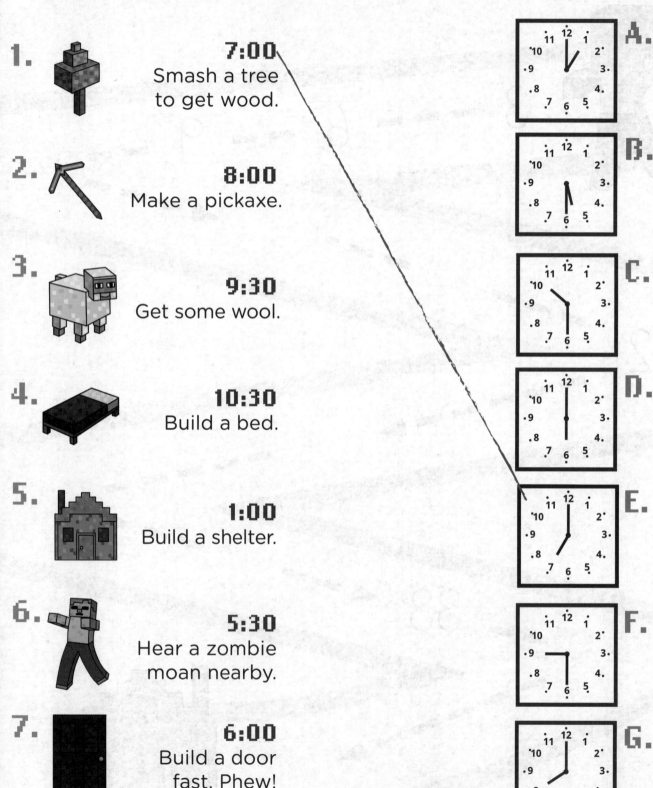

1. **7:00**
Smash a tree
to get wood.

2. **8:00**
Make a pickaxe.

3. **9:30**
Get some wool.

4. **10:30**
Build a bed.

5. **1:00**
Build a shelter.

6. **5:30**
Hear a zombie
moan nearby.

7. **6:00**
Build a door
fast. Phew!

A.
B.
C.
D.
E.
F.
G.

TIME FOR CLOCKS

Draw a big hand and a little hand on the clock to show the time.

Example:

5:00

2:30

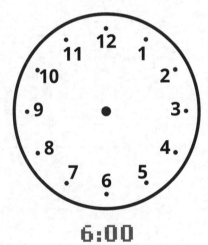

6:00

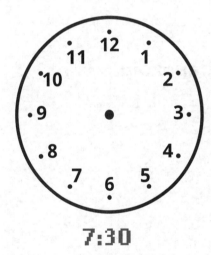

7:30

11:00

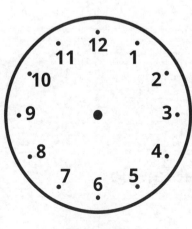

12:30

LEARNING ABOUT SHAPES

Draw along the dotted line to complete each shape. Connect the name of the shape to the correct drawing.

1. triangle

2. trapezoid

3. square

4. rectangle

A.

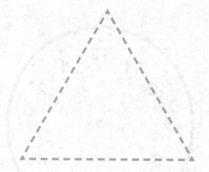

B.

C.

D.

FIND THE SHAPES

Look at the items below and and use the word box to write the name:

square	circle	rectangle

5.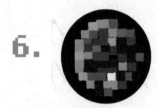

6.

7.

8. HARDCORE MODE: *Try this hardcore math challenge!*
Find 7 triangles in this pile of diamonds and circle them.

ADDITION BY GROUPING

Circle groups of 10 weapons and tools. Then count and write the total number.

Example:

1.

Answer: ___14___

2.

Answer: _____

3.

Answer: _____

4.

Answer: _____

MYSTERY MESSAGE
WITH ADDITION AND SUBTRACTION

Add or subtract. Then use the letters to fill in the blanks below and reveal the answer to Steve's joke.

1. $12 + 8 =$ 20 B

2. $11 - 8 =$ _____ A

3. $19 - 3 =$ _____ L

4. $14 + 3 =$ _____ Y

5. $11 + 2 =$ _____ K

6. $18 - 7 =$ _____ T

7. $12 - 3 =$ _____ P

8. $13 - 5 =$ _____ R

9. $17 - 5 =$ _____ O

10. $15 - 9 =$ _____ C

Q: What kind of party do Minecrafters throw?

COPY THE LETTERS FROM THE ANSWERS ABOVE TO FIND OUT.

B _____ _____ _____ _____
20   16   12   6   13

_____ _____ _____ _____ _____
9   3   8   11   17

THE ENDER DRAGON NUMBER CHALLENGE

Match the Ender Dragon with the description of the number.

1.

Tens	Ones
7	6

A. 31

2.

Tens	Ones
1	7

B. 64

3.

Tens	Ones
6	4

C. 98

4.

Tens	Ones
3	1

D. 76

5.

Tens	Ones
9	8

E. 17

SKIP COUNT CHALLENGE

Count by 5s to help tame the cat. Feed it enough fish on this numbered path and you'll have a new pet!

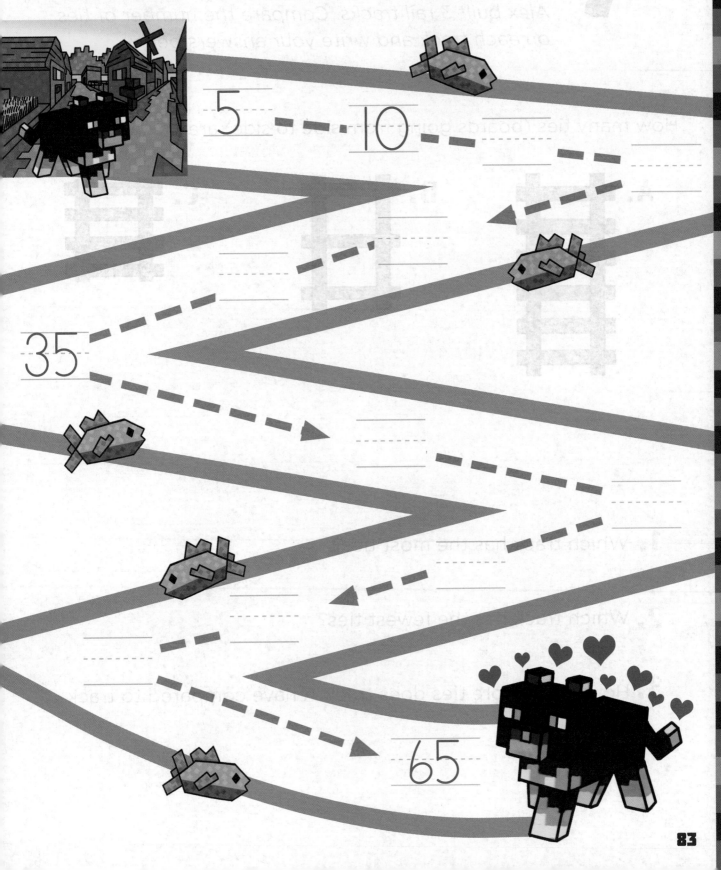

5 ----- 10

35

65

COMPARING RAIL TRACKS

Alex built 3 rail tracks. Compare the number of ties on each track and write your answers below.

How many ties (boards going from side to side) are on each track?

A.
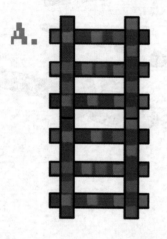

B.
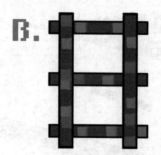

C.
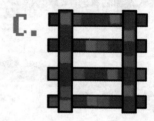

_____   _____   _____

- -

_____   _____   _____

1. Which track has the most ties?

2. Which track has the fewest ties?

3. How many more ties does track A have compared to track C?

_____ **ties.**

4. Draw your own rail track, called rail track D, in the space below. It must have more ties than rail track C, but less than rail track A. Color it in and add a rail cart full of loot!

D.

5. How many ties does your track have? _____

6. Fill in the rest of this table to keep track of all the different tracks.

Track	Number of Ties
A	6
B	
C	
D	

ADVENTURES IN GEOMETRY

Trace the dotted line to divide these shapes into 2 equal parts. Then color one half (½) of the shape.

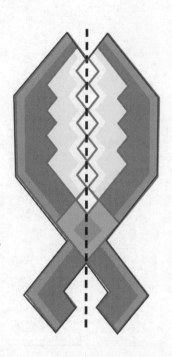

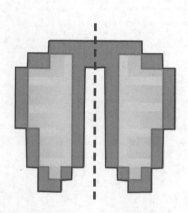

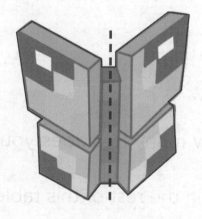

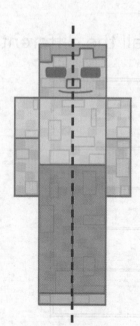

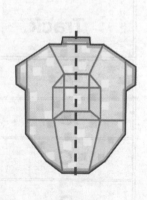

Trace the dotted line to divide these shapes into 4 equal parts. Then color in one fourth (¼) of each shape below.

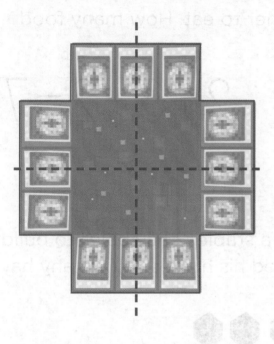

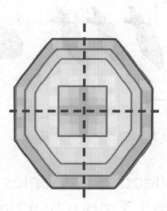

Color in one third of this wooden plank:

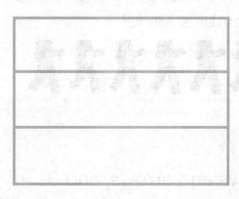

⅓

Color in three fourths of this wooden plank:

¾

WORD PROBLEMS

Read the problem carefully. Look at the picture and fill in your answer.

Example:

1. Alex eats 2 carrots. She attacks zombies, and they drop 3 more carrots and 2 potatoes for her to eat. How many food items does she eat all together?

$$2 + 3 + 2 = 7$$

Answer: 7

2. Steve collects 5 hay bales to build a stable, 2 hay bales to build a barn, and 3 more hay bales to feed his horses. How many hay bales does he have in all?

Answer: _____

3. Steve sees 15 zombies on his adventures. He destroys 5 with a trap and 6 more with his sword. How many zombies are left?

Answer: _____

4. In one day, Alex makes 7 swords, 3 bows and arrows, and 8 shovels to attack mobs. How many weapons did she make in all?

Answer: _____

5. Alex gets 4 cookies from trading with a villager. She gets 6 more cookies later in the day and 2 more cookies in the morning. How many cookies does she have in all?

Answer: _____

6. You start your game with 18 hunger points. You lose 3 points running away from a ghast. You lose 5 more points attacking skeletons. How many hunger points are left?

Answer: _____

7. You start your game with 8 items in your inventory. You remove 3 tools and 2 food items. How many items are left in your inventory?

Answer: _____

8. Steve loves his pet cats. He has 3 in a fenced area outside, 5 in his house, and 4 in another fenced area. How many pet cats does he have?

Answer: _____

PIG'S GUIDE TO PLACE VALUE

Use the number below each pig to fill in the place value chart.

Example:

1.

Hundreds	Tens	Ones
1	7	9

179

2.  **235**

Hundreds	Tens	Ones

3.  **467**

Hundreds	Tens	Ones

4. **596**

Hundreds	Tens	Ones

5. **708**

Hundreds	Tens	Ones

6.  **430**

Hundreds	Tens	Ones

7. **264**

Hundreds	Tens	Ones

SKIP COUNT CHALLENGE

Fill in the blank spaces as you count from 110 to 125 and help the horse find her way back to the barn.

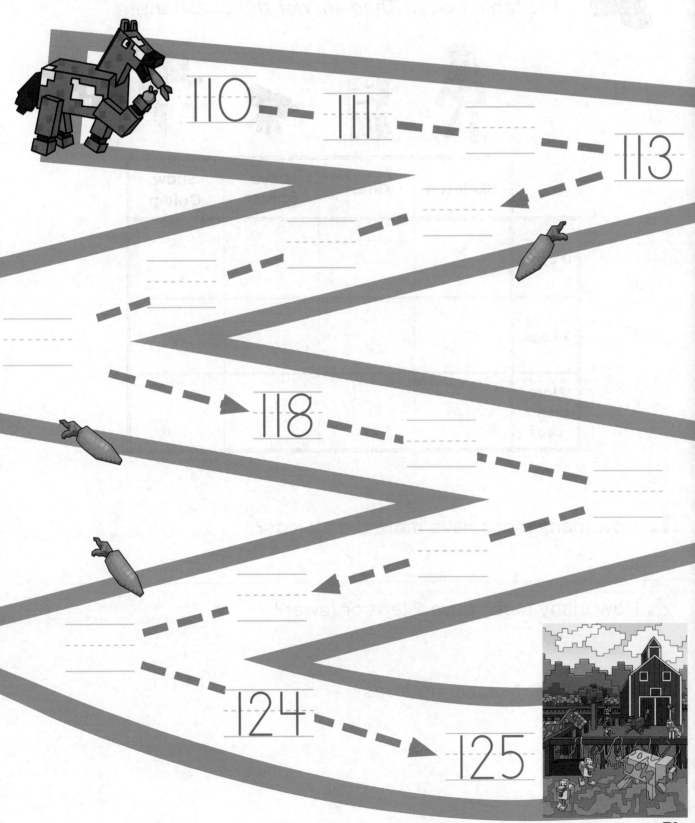

110 --- 111 --- ___ --- 113

___ --- ___ --- ___

___ --- 118 --- ___

___ --- ___ --- ___

___ --- 124 --- 125

MOBS AND MONSTERS

Video game characters are sometimes called mobs. Add an X to the boxes that describe each mob in the table below. Then answer the questions.

	Skeleton	Ghast	Cave Spider	Snow Golem
0 Legs				
2 Legs				
More than 2 Legs				

1. How many mobs have more than 2 legs? _____

2. How many mobs have 2 legs or fewer? _____

3. Which 2 mobs have no arms?

_____

_____

COUNTING MONEY

Steve wants to feed his farm animals the following items. Find out how much money each item costs and write the amount in the space provided.

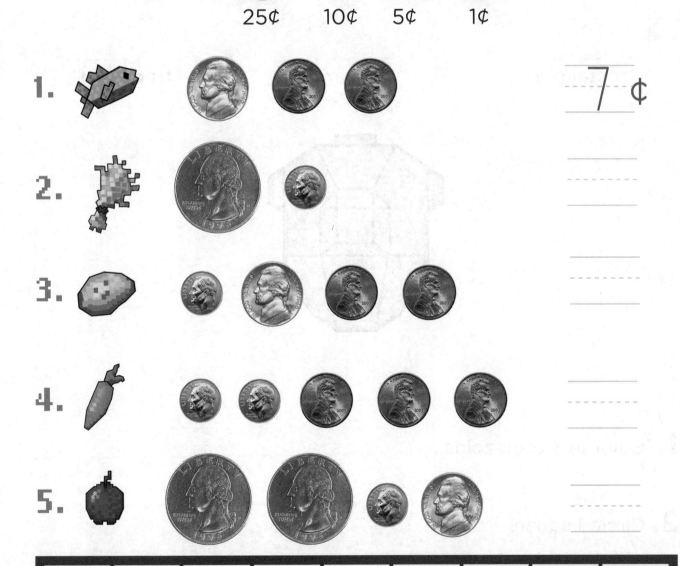

1. _7_ ¢

2. _____

3. _____

4. _____

5. _____

HARDCORE MODE: *Try this hardcore math challenge!*

6. How much money does Steve need to buy 2 fish and 3 carrots? Add them up to find out!

Answer: _____

ADVENTURES IN GEOMETRY: SPOT THE SHAPES

Look at the diamond chestplate and answer the questions.
Use the shapes below to help you.

rectangle

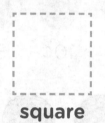
square

trapezoid

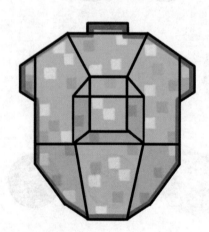

1. Color in 3 trapezoids.

2. Circle 1 square.

3. Place an x inside 2 rectangles.

CREATIVE MODE
Use a pencil or pen to change the square into 2 triangles!

Draw Alex wearing a chestplate like this one.
Use as many shapes as you can. Add fun
details and color!

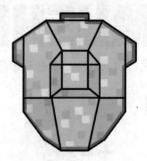

MUSHROOM ADDITION

Add the ones and then the tens to get the answer.

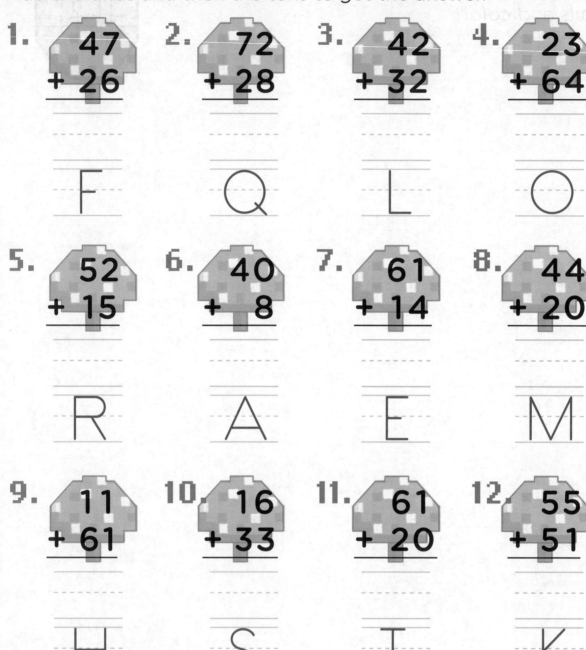

1. 47
  + 26
  _____

  F

2. 72
  + 28
  _____

  Q

3. 42
  + 32
  _____

  L

4. 23
  + 64
  _____

  O

5. 52
  + 15
  _____

  R

6. 40
  + 8
  _____

  A

7. 61
  + 14
  _____

  E

8. 44
  + 20
  _____

  M

9. 11
  + 61
  _____

  H

10. 16
  + 33
  _____

  S

11. 61
  + 20
  _____

  T

12. 55
  + 51
  _____

  K

HIDDEN MESSAGE:

Odd numbers end in 1, 3, 5, 7, or 9. Circle the ODD numbered answers above. Write the letter from those blocks in order from left to right below to spell out the name of a biome with lots of mushrooms:

_____   _____   _____   _____

_____   _____   _____   _____

SUBTRACTION MYSTERY MESSAGE

Subtract the ones, then the tens. Use the letters to fill in the blanks below and answer Alex's riddle.

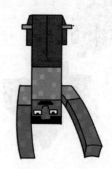

1. 45
   − 21
   _____

   Y

2. 77
   − 45
   _____

   C

3. 93
   − 20
   _____

   O

4. 26
   − 12
   _____

   B

5. 32
   − 10
   _____

   U

6. 94
   − 13
   _____

   E

7. 48
   − 27
   _____

   A

8. 74
   − 23
   _____

   R

9. 68
   − 23
   _____

   M

10. 89
    − 33
    _____

    G

Q: What's the most popular ride at the *Minecraft* carnival? Copy the letters from the answers above to find out!

___ ___ ___ ___ ___ ___ -
21   45   81   51   51   24

___ ___ - ___ ___ ___ ___
56   73   32   22   14   81

97

BOSS MOB SHOWDOWN

Who has more attack power? Compare the number of times each mob has attacked a player and write in the correct symbol.

> means greater than   **<** means less than

Example **1.**  385 **<** 391

2. 856 _____ 831

3.  445 _____ 467

4. 523 _____ 532

5. 672 _____ 668

6. 989 _____ 998

7. 723 _____ 772

Count up their wins and circle the one with the most wins below.

Wither   **Elder Guardian**

SKIP COUNT CHALLENGE

Count by 4s to help the pufferfish swim down the river and back to the ocean.

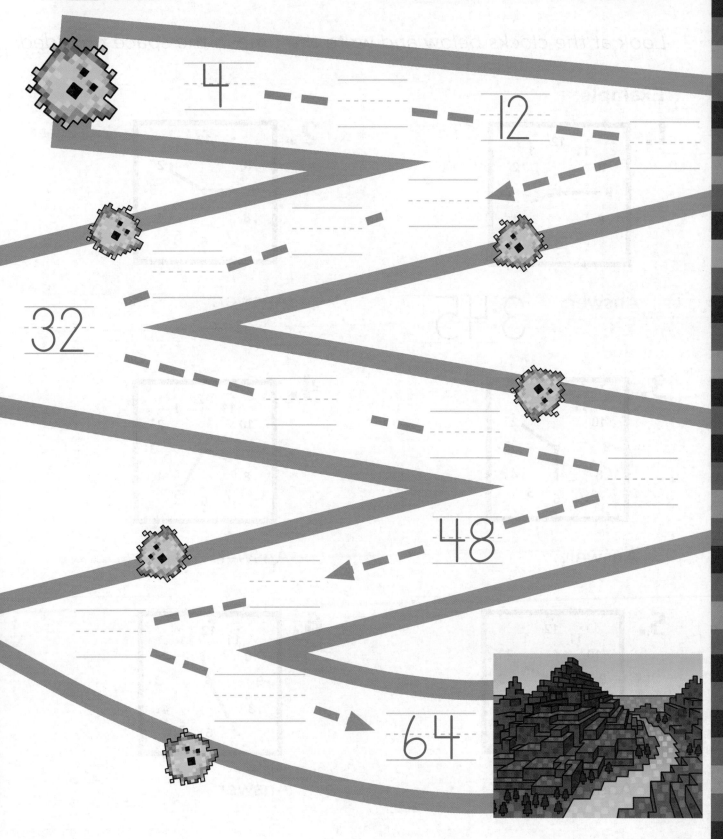

4 ___ ___ 12 ___ ___

___ ___ ___

32 ___ ___ ___

___ ___ 48

___ ___ ___ 64

TELLING TIME

 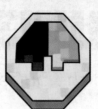  

Look at the clocks below and write the time in the space provided:

Example:

1.

Answer: 3:45

2.

Answer: _____

3.

Answer: _____

4.

Answer: _____

5.

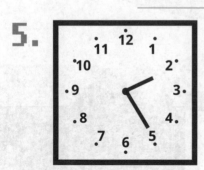

Answer: _____

6.

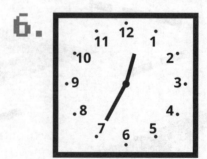

Answer: _____

7.

Answer: _____

8.

Answer: _____

9.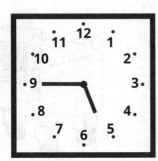

Answer: _____

10.

Answer: _____

11.

Answer: _____

12.

Answer: _____

13.

Answer: _____

14.

Answer: _____

4 SIDES ARE BETTER THAN 1

A Minecrafter's world is full of **quadrilaterals**. Find them and circle them below.

> **Hint:**
>
> Quadrilaterals are closed shapes with 4 sides.
> Squares and rectangles are two kinds of quadrilaterals.

Can you find 3 quadrilaterals on this sheep?

...5 quadrilaterals in this potion bottle?

...6 quadrilaterals in this tree?

Trace the quadrilaterals below:

ADDITION & SUBTRACTION MYSTERY NUMBER

There is a number hidden behind these lava blocks. Subtract or count on to find the mystery number.

1.
```
  15
+ ◆
────
  20
```
◆ = 5

2.
```
  22
+ ◆
────
  29
```
◆ = _____

3.
```
  43
+ ◆
────
  53
```
◆ = _____

4.
```
  17
+ ◆
────
  25
```
◆ = _____

5.
```
  76
+ ◆
────
  82
```
◆ = _____

6.
```
  50
+ ◆
────
  64
```
◆ = _____

7.
```
  49
+ ◆
────
  56
```
◆ = _____

8.
```
  27
+ ◆
────
  30
```
◆ = _____

9.
```
  63
+ ◆
────
  70
```
◆ = _____

MYSTERY MESSAGE
WITH ADDITION USING REGROUPING

Add. Use the letters to fill in the blanks below and answer the riddle.

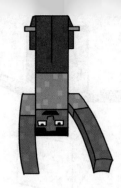

1. 45
   + 16
   _____
     O

2. 36
   + 7
   _____
     V

3. 48
   + 8
   _____
     C

4. 59
   + 13
   _____
     E

5. 38
   + 7
   _____
     I

6. 25
   + 9
   _____
     W

7. 46
   + 25
   _____
     R

8. 66
   + 19
   _____
     L

9. 28
   + 24
   _____
     S

10. 47
   + 16
   _____
     A

Q: What happened when Steve accidentally ate a bunch of rocks?

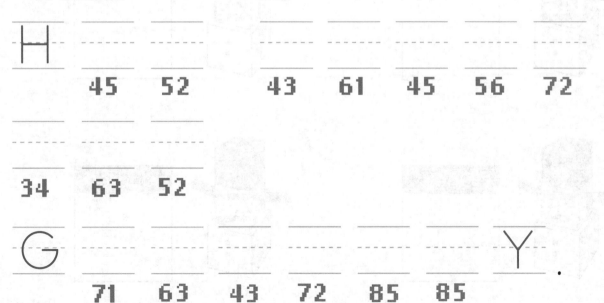

H __ __   __ __ __ __ __
  45 52   43 61 45 56 72

__ __ __
34 63 52

G __ __ __ __ __ __ Y .
  71 63 43 72 85 85

SNOW GOLEM'S GUIDE TO PLACE VALUE

Identify the number that belongs in the place-value chart and write it there.

Example:

1.

Tens
3

2.

Hundreds

3.

Ones

4.

Hundreds

5.

Tens

6.

Ones

7.

Hundreds

SKIP COUNT CHALLENGE

Count by 6s to help Alex ride the runaway pig back to the pen where it belongs.

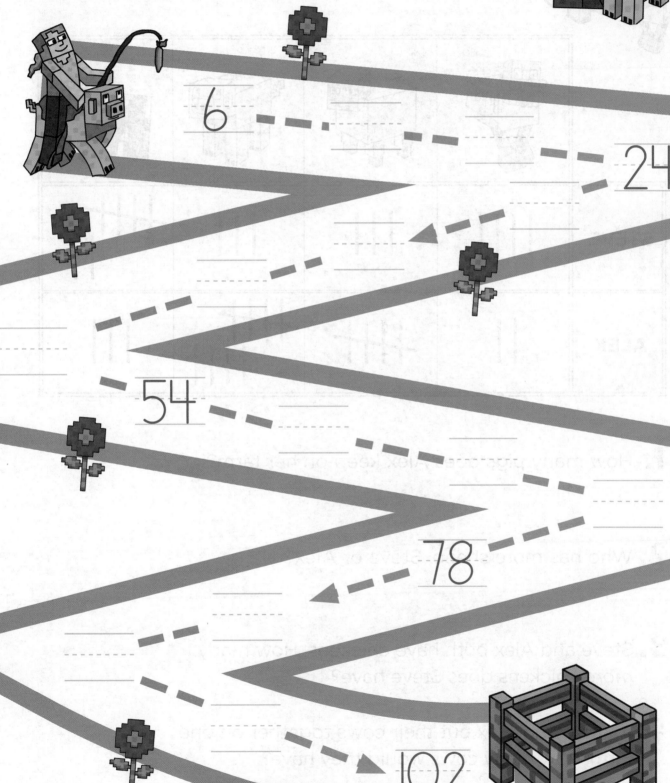

6

24

54

78

102

ANIMAL TALLY

Use the table to compare the animals that Alex and Steve have on their farms.

STEVE	IIII	III	III	Ħ II
ALEX	II	Ħ	Ħ Ħ	III

1. How many pigs does Alex keep on her farm?

2. Who has more sheep, Steve or Alex?

3. Steve and Alex both have chickens. How many *more* chickens does Steve have?

4. If Steve and Alex put their cows together on one farm, how many cows would they have?

108

WEAPON TALLY

Use the table to compare the weapons that Steve and Alex have crafted.

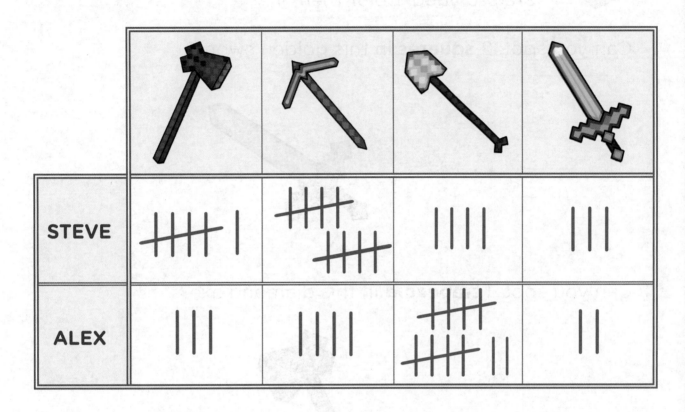

STEVE	~~||||~~ |	~~||||~~ ~~||||~~	||||	|||
ALEX	|||	||||	~~||||~~ ~~||||~~ ||	||

1. How many diamond swords did Alex craft? ....

2. Steve and Alex both have pickaxes. How many *more* pickaxes does Steve have? ....

3. Steve and Alex both have shovels. How many *more* shovels does Alex have? ....

4. Who has the most axes? ....

ADVENTURES IN GEOMETRY: SPOT THE SHAPES

Identify and circle the shapes. Examples of each shape are provided. Color them in.

1. Can you spot: 2 **squares** in this golden sword?

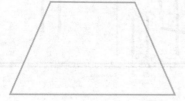

2. Can you spot: 1 **trapezoid** in this diamond axe?

3. Can you spot 2 **rectangles** in these iron bars?

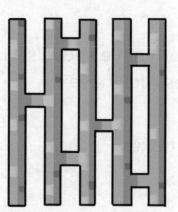

Match the name of the shape to the correct object.

1. Octagon

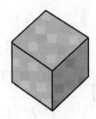 **A.**

2. Quadrilateral

 **B.**

3. Oval

 **C.**

4. Sphere

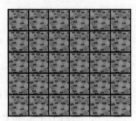 **D.**

5. Cube

 E.

WORD PROBLEMS

Write a number sentence to help you solve these word problems.

Example:

1. You break 12 dirt blocks with your diamond shovel. You also break 4 sand blocks and 6 gravel blocks. How many blocks do you break in all?

12 + 4 + 6 = 22

Answer: 22 blocks

2. Your pumpkin pie has 12 slices. You eat 2 slices, your friend eats 3 slices, and you feed 1 slice to your pet cat. How many slices are left?

Answer: _____

3. You plant 8 flowers in your yard. A goat comes along and eats 3 of them. You plant 5 more. How many flowers do you have now?

Answer: _____

4. You grow 3 potatoes. The next day you grow 5 new potatoes. How many potatoes do you have in all?

Answer:

5. You destroy Endermen and collect 25 Eyes of Ender. You use 13 to activate the End Portal. How many Eyes of Ender do you have left?

Answer:

6. You want to make a diamond suit of armor. The helmet requires 5 diamonds, the chestplate requires 8 diamonds, and the leggings require 7 diamonds. How many diamonds do you need in all?

Answer:

7. Your house is made of 30 cobblestone blocks. An Enderman steals 12 blocks from your house. The next night, he steals 6 more blocks. How many blocks are left?

Answer:

SKELETON'S GUIDE TO PLACE VALUE

Match the number on each skeleton to the place value descriptions on the right.

Example:

1.

367

Tens
6

2.

451

Ones

3.

734

Tens

4.

890

Ones

5.

625

Hundreds

6.

307

Tens

7.

824

Hundreds

SKIP COUNT CHALLENGE

Count by 100s to fill in the path and help tame this wolf with bones.

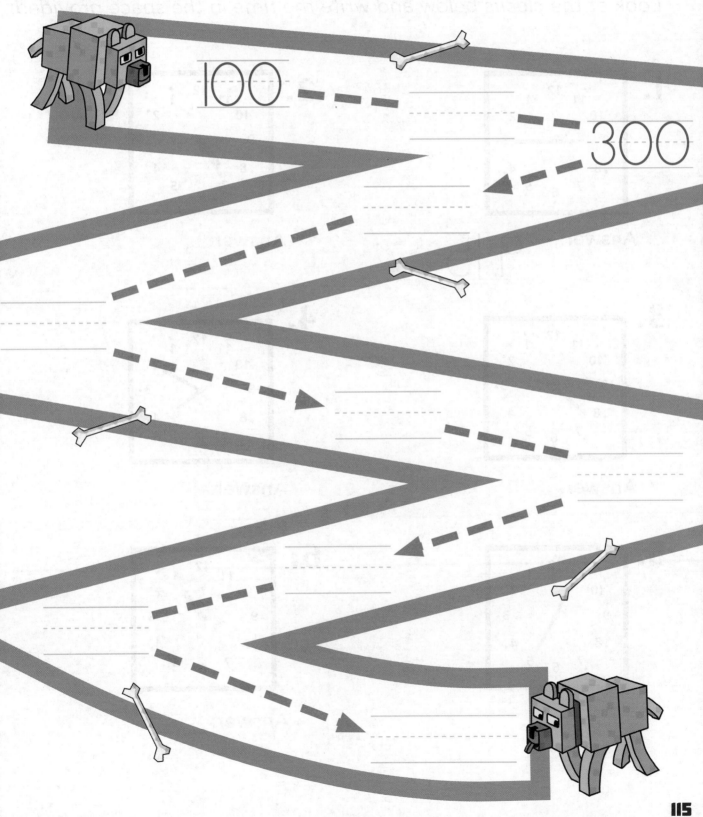

100

300

TELLING TIME

Look at the clocks below and write the time in the space provided:

1.

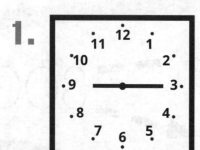

Answer: 9:15

2.

Answer: _____

3.

Answer: _____

4.

Answer: _____

5.

Answer: _____

6.

Answer: _____

COUNTING MONEY

How much money is hidden in each treasure chest? Add up the coins to find out.

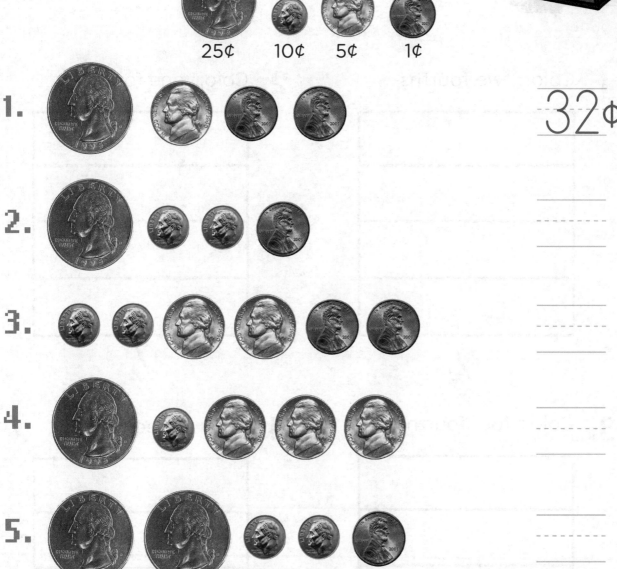

25¢   10¢   5¢   1¢

1.   32¢

2.

3.

4.

5.

HARDCORE MODE: Try this hardcore math challenge!
Steve looks in a treasure chest and finds 5 coins that add up
to 25¢. There is only 1 kind of coin in the treasure chest.
What coin is it?

GEOMETRY

This wooden plank is divided into 4 equal parts called fourths (or quarters). Color the wooden planks below according to the description.

1. Color: two fourths

2/4

2. Color: one fourth

1/4

3. Color: four fourths

4/4

4. Color: three fourths

3/4

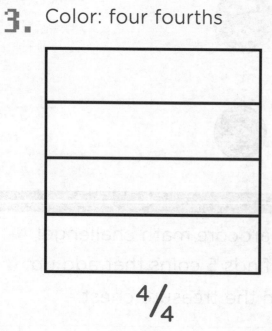

Match the shaded set of blocks to the correct fraction on the right.

5. 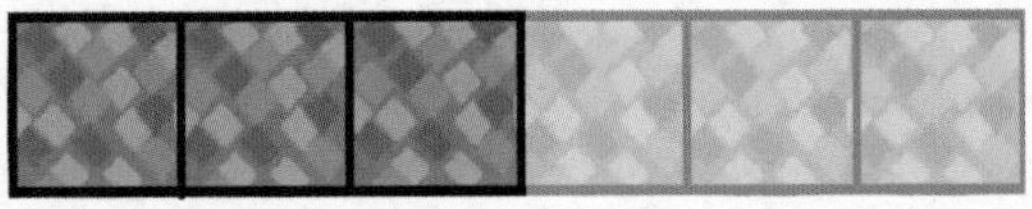 $\dfrac{5}{6}$

6. 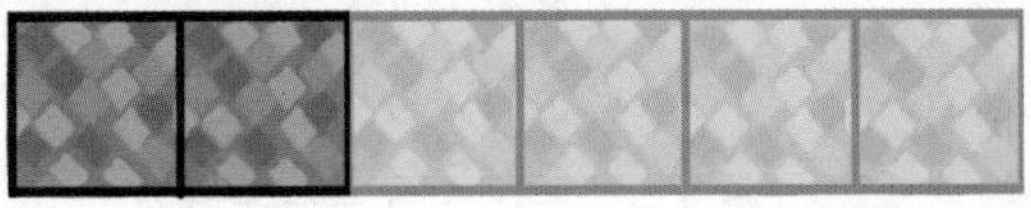 $\dfrac{3}{6}$

7. 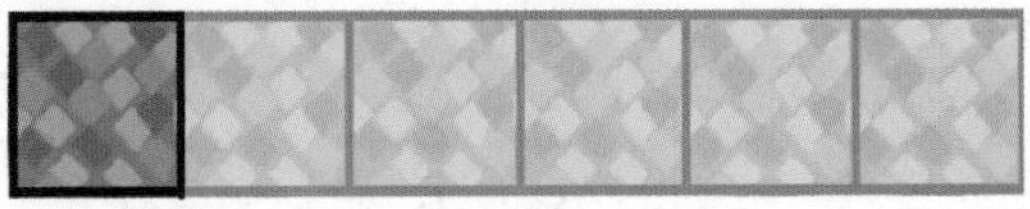 $\dfrac{2}{6}$

8. 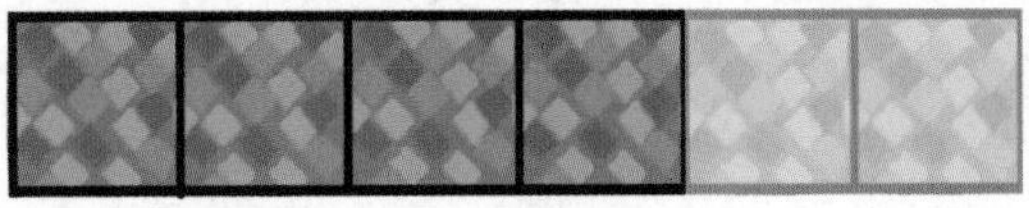 $\dfrac{4}{6}$

9. 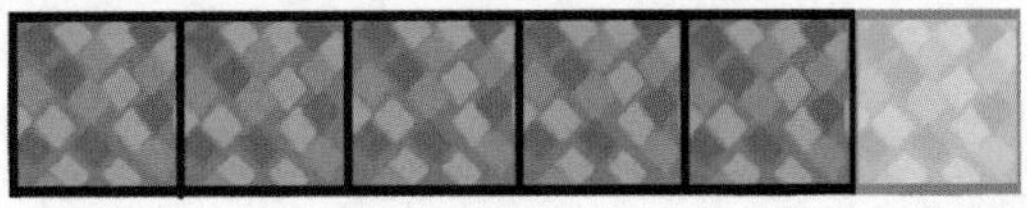 $\dfrac{1}{6}$

ANSWER KEY

Page 8
1. 5
2. 3
3. 6
4. 9
5. 4

Page 9
1. 8
2. 7
3. 5
4. 10
5. 14
6. 4
7. 12
8. 3
9. 15

Minecraft

Page 10
1. 5
2. 5
3. 7
4. 5
5. 8
6. 7
7. 7
8. 8
9. 10
10. 10

Page 11
2, 4, 6, 8, 10, 12, 14, 16, 18, 20

Page 12
1. 2
2. 5
3. 2
4. 3
5. 0
6. 4

Page 13
1. 2
2. 3
3. 2
4. 3
5. 4
6. 1

Page 14
1. 4, IIII
2. 7, IIII II
3. 6, IIII I
4. 5, IIII
5. 3, III
6. 8, IIII III

Page 15
1. 3, III
2. 4, IIII
3. 5, IIII
4. 1, I
5. 6, IIII I
6. 7, IIII II

Page 16
1. 7
2. 9
3. 10
4. 5
5. 8
6. 4

Page 17
1. 5
2. 7
3. 3
4. 9
5. 8
6. 1
7. 6
8. 2

A skeleton

Page 18
1. 5
2. 3
3. 5
4. 6
5. 1
6. 0
7. 4
8. 9

Page 19
3, 6, 9, 12, 15, 18, 21, 24, 27, 30

Page 20
1. 3
2. 6
3. 5
4. 0
5. 4
6. 7
7. 8
8. 6

Page 21
Monster egg

Page 22
1. 10
2. 10
3. 10
4. 10
5. 10
6. 10
7. 10
8. 10
9. 10
10. 10

Page 23

1. 2
2. 4
3. 3
4. 5
5. 7
6. 6
7. 9
8. 10
9. 1
10. 8

Page 24

1. 1
2. 2
3. 2
4. 3
5. 3
6. 4
7. 4
8. 5
9. 5
10. 6
11. 6
12. 7
13. 7
14. 8
15. 8
16. 9
17. 9
18. 10
19. 10
20. 11

Page 25

1. 3
2. 4
3. 4
4. 5
5. 5
6. 6
7. 6
8. 7
9. 7
10. 8
11. 8
12. 9
13. 9
14. 10
15. 10
16. 9
17. 7
18. 7
19. 2
20. 3

Page 26

1. 2 tens, 7 ones
2. 1 ten, 6 ones
3. 4 tens, 6 ones
4. 0 tens, 8 ones
5. 6 tens, 2 ones
6. 8 tens, 0 ones

Page 27

4, 8, 12, 16, 20, 24, 28, 32, 36, 40

Page 28

1. 4 wooden planks
2. 7 iron swords
3. 8 carrots
4. 6 melons

Page 29

1. 5 diamond blocks
2. 5 TNT blocks
3. 2 eggs
4. 5 wooden swords

Page 30

1. 6
2. 7
3. 9
4. 5
5. 9
6. 10
7. 7
8. 8

When you add an even number to an even number, the answer is even.

When you add an even number to an odd number, the answer is odd.

Page 31

1. 6
2. 4
3. 7
4. 3
5. 4
6. 1
7. 5
8. 2

When you subtract an even number from an even number, the answer is even.

When you subtract an even number from an odd number, the answer is odd.

Page 32
1. 5
2. 6
3. 6
4. 7
5. 7
6. 8
7. 8
8. 9
9. 9
10. 10
11. 10
12. 11
13. 11
14. 12
15. 12
16. 13
17. 13
18. 14
19. 14
20. 15

Page 33
1. 3 + 4 = 7
   4 + 3 = 7
2. 5 + 3 = 8
   3 + 5 = 8
3. 7 + 2 = 9
   2 + 7 = 9
4. 8 + 1 = 9
   1 + 8 = 9
5. 4 + 5 = 9
   5 + 4 = 9
6. 10 + 0 = 10
   0 + 10 = 10

The answers in each pair are the same no matter which number comes first.

Page 34
1. 9
2. 8
3. 5
4. 0
5. 2
6. 0
7. 6
8. 3

Page 35
5, 10, 15, 20, 25, 30, 35, 40, 45, 50

Page 36
1. 7 diamond blocks
2. 11 torches
3. 10 plants
4. 12 red mushrooms

Page 37
1. 3 tools
2. 5 plants
3. 8 horses
4. 7 pumpkin pies

Page 38
1. 15; 1 ten 5 ones
2. 12; 1 ten, 2 ones
3. 14; 1 ten, 4 ones
4. 20; 2 tens, 0 ones
5. 13; 1 ten, 3 ones
6. 20; 2 tens, 0 ones

Page 39
1. 9; 0 tens, 9 ones
2. 6; 0 tens, 6 ones
3. 10; 1 ten, 0 ones
4. 7; 0 tens, 7 ones
5. 16; 1 ten, 6 ones
6. 0; 0 tens, 0 ones

Page 40
1. 8
2. 4
3. 4
4. 3
5. 0
6. 6
7. 4
8. 7
9. 3
10. 1
11. 5
12. 5
13. 2
14. 5
15. 4
16. 2
17. 7
18. 3
19. 5
20. 2

Page 41
1. 6
2. 3
3. 5
4. 3
5. 1
6. 8
7. 4
8. 2
9. 7
10. 3
11. 3
12. 8
13. 4
14. 2
15. 4
16. 4
17. 6
18. 8
19. 4
20. 5

Page 42

1. 6 hundreds, 2 tens, 9 ones
2. 7 hundreds, 0 tens, 8 ones
3. 3 hundred, 1 tens, 9 ones
4. 8 hundreds, 3 tens, 0 ones
5. 9 hundreds, 8 tens, 5 ones
6. 3 hundreds, 0 tens, 4 ones

Page 43

6, 12, 18, 24, 30, 36, 42, 48, 54, 60

Page 44

1. 5
2. 7
3. 8
4. 10
5. 14
6. 6
7. 6
8. 15
9. 9

Page 45

Killer Bunny

Page 46

1. 90 + 1
2. 70 + 6
3. 40 + 3
4. 80 + 5
5. 30 + 9
6. 60 + 0

Page 47

1. 300 + 20 + 4
2. 800 + 40 + 9
3. 600 + 70 + 0
4. 500 + 00 + 6
5. 900 + 30 + 2
6. 400 + 80 + 1

Page 48

1. 17
2. 34
3. 7
4. 23
5. 13
6. 26

Page 49

1. 18
2. 17
3. 6
4. 19
5. 15
6. 7
7. 13
8. 12

A slverfsh

Page 50

1. 6
2. 7
3. 0
4. 9
5. 7
6. 0
7. 6
8. 1

Page 51

7, 14, 21, 28, 35, 42, 49, 56, 63, 70

Page 52

1. 16
2. 10
3. 13
4. 0
5. 14
6. 17
7. 11
8. 19
9. 12

Page 53

A night-mare

Page 54

1. 46
2. 29
3. 75
4. 88
5. 57
6. 62
7. 14
8. 37

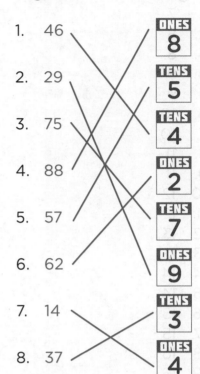

Page 55

1. 24
2. 30
3. 42
4. 12
5. 66
6. 57
7. 81
8. 39

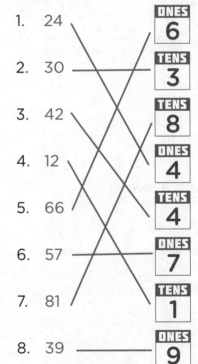

Page 56

1. 7
2. 8
3. 8
4. 9
5. 9
6. 10
7. 10
8. 11
9. 11
10. 12
11. 12
12. 13
13. 13
14. 14
15. 14
16. 15
17. 15
18. 16
19. 16
20. 17

Page 57

1. 11
2. 20
3. 8
4. 19
5. 10
6. 5
7. 15
8. 7

I am a sword

Page 54

1. 11
2. 11
3. 8
4. 11
5. 16
6. 7
7. 12
8. 18
9. 8
10. 14
11. 14
12. 8
13. 13
14. 12
15. 6
16. 11
17. 3
18. 13
19. 8
20. 15

Page 59

8, 16, 24, 32, 40, 48, 56, 64, 72, 80

Page 60

1. 9 blocks
2. 12 swords
3. 15 crops
4. 16 mobs

Page 61

1. 12 blocks
2. 11 fish
3. 3 ocelots
4. 6 skeletons

Page 62

1. 13; 1 ten, 3 ones
2. 12; 1 ten, 2 ones
3. 15; 1 ten, 5 ones
4. 20; 2 tens, 0 ones
5. 16; 1 ten, 6 ones
6. 20; 2 tens, 0 ones

Page 63

1. 7; 0 tens, 7 ones
2. 6; 0 tens, 6 ones
3. 10; 1 tens, 0 ones
4. 5; 0 tens, 5 ones
5. 13; 1 tens, 3 ones
6. 9; 0 tens, 9 ones

Page 64

2. 13
3. 26
4. 17
5. 15

Page 65

2. 6
3. 14
4. 11
5. 7
6. 16
7. 5
8. 13
A: FACEBLOCK

Page 66

2. 3 tens 7 ones
3. 4 tens 1 ones
4. 7 tens 2 ones
5. 6 tens 3 ones
6. 5 tens 0 ones
7. 9 tens 8 ones

Page 67

6, 8, 10, 12, 14, 16, 20, 22, 24, 26

Page 68

2. 5:30
3. 10:00
4. 7:30
5. 1:30
6. 6:00

Page 69

2. 21 cents
3. 31 cents
4. 41 cents
5. 31 cents
6. 41 cents
7. 47 cents

Hardcore Mode:

8. 3 dimes

Page 70
Insert answer at the top: 4
Note: Answers may vary.

1.

2.

Page 71

3. 6

4.

5.

6. Hardcore Mode: $\frac{1}{3}$

Page 72

1. 2
2. 4
3. 3

Page 73

4. 8
5. 9
6. 3
7. 7
8. 3

Page 74

2. 2 tens, 7 ones
3. 8 tens, 6 ones
4. 3 tens, 2 ones
5. 7 tens, 1 ones
6. 6 tens, 0 ones
7. 5 tens, 4 ones

Page 75

12, 15, 18, 24, 27, 30, 36, 39

Page 76

2. G
3. F
4. C
5. A
6. B
7. D

Page 77

2.
3.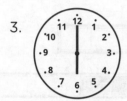
4.
5.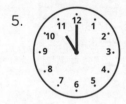
6.

Page 78

1. B
2. D
3. A
4. C

Page 79

5. Square
6. Circle
7. Rectangle

Note: Answers may vary.

8.

Page 80

2. 34
3. 23
4. 20

Page 81

2. 3
3. 16
4. 17
5. 13
6. 11
7. 9
8. 8
9. 12
10. 6

A: BLOCK PARTY

Page 82

1. D
2. E
3. B
4. A
5. C

Page 83

15, 20, 25, 30, 40, 45, 50, 55, 60

Page 84

A. 6 ties
B. 3 ties
C. 4 ties

1. A
2. B
3. 2 ties
5. 5 ties

Page 85

Note: Answers may vary.

Track	Number of Ties
A	6
B	3
C	4
D	5

Pages 86–87

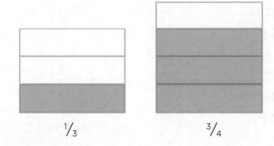

1/3   3/4

Pages 88–99

2. 10 hay bales

3. 4 zombies

4. 18 weapons

5. 12 cookies

6. 10 hunger points

7. 3 items

8. 12 pet cats

Page 90

2. Hundreds:2 Tens:3 Ones:5

3. Hundreds:4 Tens:6 Ones:7

4. Hundreds:5 Tens:9 Ones:6

5. Hundreds:7 Tens:0 Ones:8

6. Hundreds:4 Tens:3 Ones:0

7. Hundreds:2 Tens:6 Ones:4

Page 91

112, 114, 115, 116, 117, 119, 120, 121, 122, 123

Page 92

	Skeleton	Ghast	Cave Spider	Snow Golem
0 Legs				X
2 Legs	X			
More than 2 Legs		X	X	

1. 2 mobs

2. 2 mobs

3. Ghast and Cave spider

Page 93

2. 35 cents

3. 17 cents

4. 23 cents

5. 65 cents

Hardcore Mode: 6. 83 cents

Page 94

Note: Answers may vary.

Page 96

1. 73

2. 100

3. 74

4. 87

5. 67

6. 48

7. 75

8. 64

9. 72

10. 49

11. 81

12. 106

Hidden Message: FOREST

Page 97

1. 24

2. 32

3. 73

4. 14

5. 22
6. 81
7. 21
8. 51
9. 45
10. 56
A: A MERRY-GO-CUBE

Page 98
1. <
2. >
3. <
4. <
5. >
6. <
7. <
Elder Guardian

Page 99
8, 16, 20, 24, 28, 36, 40, 44, 52, 56, 60

Page 100-101
2. 9:10
3. 6:10
4. 8:25
5. 2:25
6. 12:35
7. 8:50
8. 11:40
9. 5:45
10. 12:05
11. 8:10
12. 1:45
13. 9:55
14. 3:40

Page 102

Page 104
2. 7
3. 10
4. 8
5. 6
6. 14
7. 7
8. 3
9. 7

Page 105
1. 61
2. 43
3. 56
4. 72
5. 45
6. 34
7. 71
8. 85
9. 52
10. 63
A: HIS VOICE WAS GRAVELLY.

Page 106
2. 7
3. 9
4. 1
5. 3
6. 0
7. 7

Page 107
12, 18, 30, 36, 42, 48, 60, 66, 72, 84, 90, 96

Page 108
1. 10
2. Alex
3. 2
4. 10

Page 109
1. 2
2. 6
3. 8
4. Steve

Page 110

1.

2.

3.

Page 111
1. C
2. D
3. E
4. B
5. A

Pages 112-113
2. 6 slices
3. 10 flowers
4. 8 potatoes
5. 12 Eyes of Ender
6. 20 diamonds
7. 12 cobblestone blocks

Page 114
2. 1
3. 3
4. 0
5. 6
6. 0
7. 8

Page 115
200, 400, 500, 600, 700, 800, 900, 1,000

Page 116
2. 7:35
3. 2:40
4. 4:10
5. 11:25
6. 1:05

Page 117
2. 46 cents
3. 32 cents
4. 50 cents
5. 71 cents
Hardcore Mode:
Nickel

Pages 118–119
Note: Answers may vary.

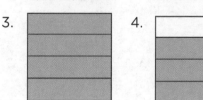

5. $^3/_6$
6. $^2/_6$
7. $^1/_6$
8. $^4/_6$
9. $^5/_6$

MULTIPLICATION AND DIVISION ACTIVITIES

MULTIPLICATION BY GROUPING

Write the multiplication sentence that matches the picture. Then solve the equation.

Example:

Answer: $\underline{}3\underline{} \times \underline{}2\underline{} = \underline{}6\underline{}$

1.

Answer: _____ x _____ = _____

2.

Answer: _____ x _____ = _____

3.

Answer: _____ x _____ = _____

4.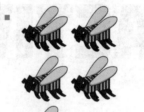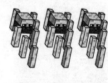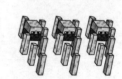

Answer: _____ x _____ = _____

MYSTERY MESSAGE WITH MULTIPLICATION

Multiply. Then use the letters to fill in the blanks below and reveal the answer to Steve's joke.

1. 3 x 9 = _____   C

2. 4 x 6 = _____   U

3. 10 x 5 = _____   I

4. 6 x 7 = _____   F

5. 7 x 5 = _____   E

6. 2 x 11 = _____   B

7. 5 x 6 = _____   J

8. 9 x 8 = _____   Y

Q: Where does Alex go to get her cart serviced?

Copy the letters from the answers above to solve the joke.

____ ____ ____ ____ ____ ____ ____ ____ ____
 30   50   42   42   72   27   24   22   35

DROWNED'S GUIDE TO PLACE VALUE

Write the number on each drowned in expanded form in the space provided.

Example:  672

Answer:

600 + 70 + 2

1.  801

2.  167

3.  450

4.  834

5.  326

6.  735

MATH FACTS CHALLENGE

Find the pattern and fill in the empty spaces to help the villager escape the skeleton.

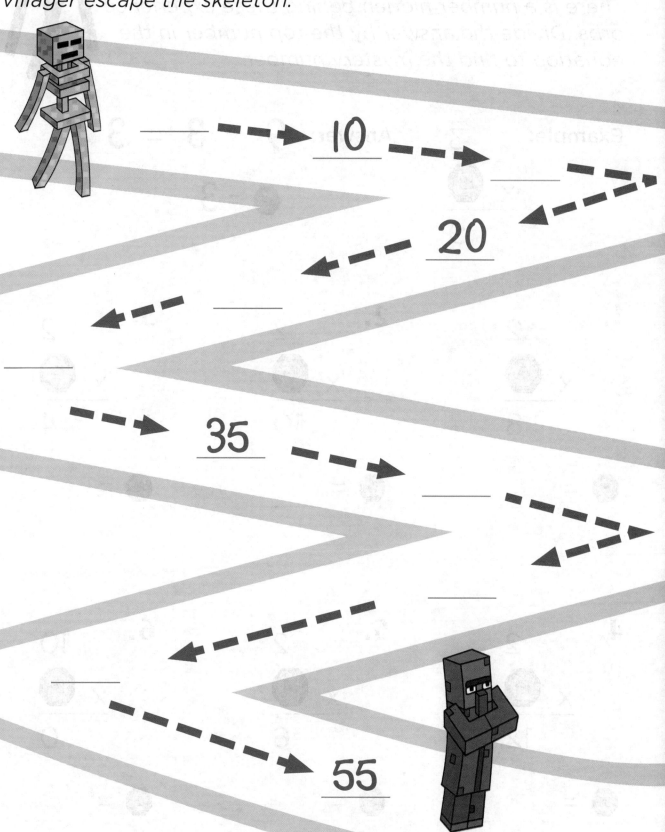

MULTIPLICATION AND DIVISION
MYSTERY NUMBER

There is a number hidden behind these experience orbs. Divide the answer by the top number in the equation to find the mystery number.

Example:

$$\begin{array}{r} 3 \\ \times \ \text{🔵} \\ \hline 9 \end{array}$$

Answer: $\underline{9} \div \underline{3} = \underline{3}$

🔵 $= 3$

1.

$$\begin{array}{r} 2 \\ \times \ \text{🔵} \\ \hline 8 \end{array}$$

🔵 $= \underline{\hspace{2cm}}$

2.

$$\begin{array}{r} 2 \\ \times \ \text{🔵} \\ \hline 10 \end{array}$$

🔵 $= \underline{\hspace{2cm}}$

3.

$$\begin{array}{r} 2 \\ \times \ \text{🔵} \\ \hline 4 \end{array}$$

🔵 $= \underline{\hspace{2cm}}$

4.

$$\begin{array}{r} 2 \\ \times \ \text{🔵} \\ \hline 12 \end{array}$$

🔵 $= \underline{\hspace{2cm}}$

5.

$$\begin{array}{r} 2 \\ \times \ \text{🔵} \\ \hline 6 \end{array}$$

🔵 $= \underline{\hspace{2cm}}$

6.

$$\begin{array}{r} 10 \\ \times \ \text{🔵} \\ \hline 0 \end{array}$$

🔵 $= \underline{\hspace{2cm}}$

MULTIPLICATION AND DIVISION
MYSTERY NUMBER

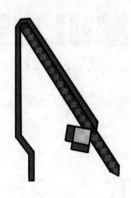

There is a number hidden behind these fish. Multiply the answer by the bottom number in the equation to find the mystery number.

Example: Answer:

$$\underline{\quad 2 \quad} \times \underline{\quad 5 \quad} = \underline{\quad 10 \quad}$$

$$\begin{array}{r} \div \quad 5 \\ \hline 2 \end{array}$$

 $= 10$

1.

$$\begin{array}{r} \div \quad 1 \\ \hline 7 \end{array}$$

 $= \underline{\qquad}$

2.

$$\begin{array}{r} \div \quad 4 \\ \hline 2 \end{array}$$

 $= \underline{\qquad}$

3.

$$\begin{array}{r} \div \quad 3 \\ \hline 2 \end{array}$$

 $= \underline{\qquad}$

4.

$$\begin{array}{r} \div \quad 5 \\ \hline 1 \end{array}$$

 $= \underline{\qquad}$

5.

$$\begin{array}{r} \div \quad 2 \\ \hline 4 \end{array}$$

 $= \underline{\qquad}$

6.

$$\begin{array}{r} \div \quad 9 \\ \hline 1 \end{array}$$

 $= \underline{\qquad}$

MULTIPLICATION IN BASE 10

Multiply the numbers. Then fill in the place value chart. The first one is done for you.

1. 8 × 7 = __56__

Tens	Ones
5	6

2. 5 × 7 = _____

Tens	Ones

3. 4 × 6 = _____

Tens	Ones

4. 9 × 7 = _____

Tens	Ones

5. 8 × 8 = _____

Tens	Ones

6. 3 × 6 = _____

Tens	Ones

7. 5 × 10 = _____

Tens	Ones

8. 3 × 9 = _____

Tens	Ones

DIVISION IN BASE 10

Divide the numbers. Then round the number up or down to the nearest ten. The first one is done for you.

Hint: Numbers 0, 1, 2, 3, and 4 round *down* to 0. Numbers 5, 6, 7, 8, and 9 round *up* to 10.

Divide	Solve it!	Round it!
1. 36 ÷ 6 =	6	10
2. 72 ÷ 9 =		
3. 24 ÷ 8 =		
4. 12 ÷ 6 =		
5. 56 ÷ 8 =		
6. 42 ÷ 7 =		
7. 10 ÷ 5 =		
8. 28 ÷ 7 =		

MULTIPLICATION BY GROUPING

Write the multiplication sentence that matches the picture. Then solve the equation. The first one is done for you.

1.

Answer: __4__ x __3__ = __12__

2.

Answer: ____ x ____ = ____

3.

Answer: ____ x ____ = ____

4.

Answer: ____ x ____ = ____

5.

Answer: ____ x ____ = ____

6.

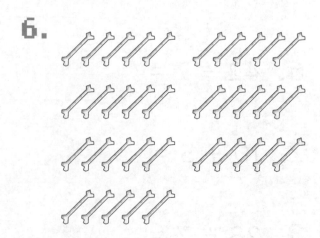

Answer: ____ x ____ = ____

MYSTERY MESSAGE WITH DIVISION

Divide. Then use the letters to fill in the blanks below and reveal the answer to Alex's riddle.

1. 18 ÷ 9 = _____ D

2. 42 ÷ 7 = _____ U

3. 50 ÷ 5 = _____ G

4. 35 ÷ 7 = _____ S

5. 81 ÷ 9 = _____ A

6. 30 ÷ 10 = _____ N

7. 56 ÷ 8 = _____ I

8. 28 ÷ 7 = _____ R

Q:What mobs make the best babysitters?

Copy the letters from the answers above to solve the joke.

_____ _____ _____ _____ _____ _____ _____ _____ _____
 10   6   9   4   2   7   9   3   5

EVOKER'S GUIDE TO PLACE VALUE

Write the correct digit in the place value chart.
The first one is done for you.

1.
 392

TENS
9

2.
 614

HUNDREDS

3.
 650

ONES

4.
 539

TENS

5.
 821

HUNDREDS

6.
 315

ONES

7.
 802

TENS

8.
 127

HUNDREDS

MATH FACTS CHALLENGE

Find the pattern and fill in the empty spaces to help Steve enchant his weapons and armor.

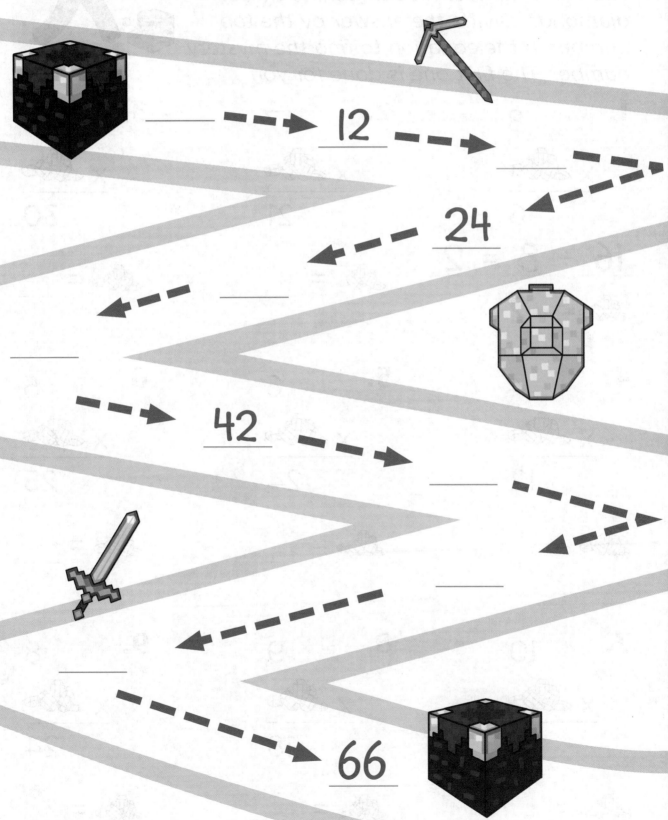

_____ → 12 → _____

24

_____

_____ → 42 →

_____

_____

_____ → 66

MULTIPLICATION AND DIVISION
MYSTERY NUMBER

There is a number hidden behind these diamonds. Divide the answer by the top number in the equation to find the mystery number. The first one is done for you.

1.

$$\begin{array}{r} 8 \\ \times \\ \hline 16 \end{array}$$

$$\underline{16} \div \underline{8} = \underline{2}$$

💎 = **2**

2.

$$\begin{array}{r} 7 \\ \times \\ \hline 21 \end{array}$$

💎 = _____

3.

$$\begin{array}{r} 6 \\ \times \\ \hline 30 \end{array}$$

💎 = _____

4.

$$\begin{array}{r} 4 \\ \times \\ \hline 12 \end{array}$$

💎 = _____

5.

$$\begin{array}{r} 6 \\ \times \\ \hline 24 \end{array}$$

💎 = _____

6.

$$\begin{array}{r} 5 \\ \times \\ \hline 25 \end{array}$$

💎 = _____

7.

$$\begin{array}{r} 10 \\ \times \\ \hline 10 \end{array}$$

💎 = _____

8.

$$\begin{array}{r} 9 \\ \times \\ \hline 18 \end{array}$$

💎 = _____

9.

$$\begin{array}{r} 8 \\ \times \\ \hline 24 \end{array}$$

💎 = _____

MULTIPLICATION AND DIVISION
MYSTERY NUMBER

There is a number hidden behind these dragon eggs. Multiply the answer by the bottom number in the equation to find the mystery number. The first one is done for you.

1.

$$\div \frac{5}{4}$$

$$\underline{4} \times \underline{5} = \underline{20}$$

 $= \underline{20}$

2.

$$\div \frac{3}{3}$$

 $= \underline{\quad}$

3.

$$\div \frac{2}{5}$$

$= \underline{\quad}$

4.

$$\div \frac{8}{2}$$

 $= \underline{\quad}$

5.

$$\div \frac{4}{5}$$

 $= \underline{\quad}$

6.

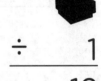

$$\div \frac{1}{12}$$

$= \underline{\quad}$

7.

$$\div \frac{6}{4}$$

 $= \underline{\quad}$

8.

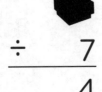

$$\div \frac{7}{4}$$

 $= \underline{\quad}$

9.

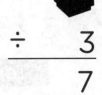

$$\div \frac{3}{7}$$

 $= \underline{\quad}$

MULTIPLICATION IN BASE 10

Multiply the numbers. Then fill in the place value chart. The first one is done for you.

1. 4 × 8 = __32__

Tens	Ones
3	2

2. 6 × 5 = _____

Tens	Ones

3. 3 × 3 = _____

Tens	Ones

4. 4 × 6 = _____

Tens	Ones

5. 4 × 5 = _____

Tens	Ones

6. 2 × 8 = _____

Tens	Ones

7. 3 × 9 = _____

Tens	Ones

8. 4 × 9 = _____

Tens	Ones

MULTIPLICATION FACTS WITH BASE 10

Multiply the numbers. Then answer the questions.

1. 1 × 10 = _____

2. 3 × 10 = _____

3. 6 × 10 = _____

4. 2 × 10 = _____

5. 5 × 10 = _____

6. 8 × 10 = _____

7. 9 × 10 = _____

8. 7 × 10 = _____

9. 10 × 10 = _____

10. 4 × 10 = _____

Q: What pattern do you notice when you multiply a one-digit number by 10?

A: _____

Q: What pattern do you think would happen when you multiply a two-digit number by 10? Test your theory below.

A: _____

Example:

10 × 10 = _____

MULTIPLICATION BY GROUPING

Write the multiplication sentence that matches the picture.
Then solve the equation. The first one is done for you.

1.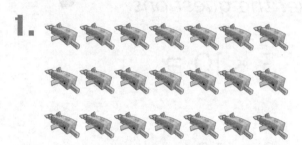

Answer: ___3___ x ___7___ = ___21___

2.

Answer: ___ x ___ = ___

3.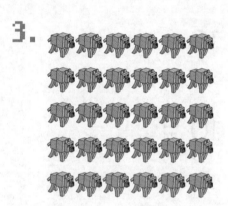

Answer: ___ x ___ = ___

4.

Answer: ___ x ___ = ___

5.

Answer: ___ x ___ = ___

6.

Answer: ___ x ___ = ___

7.

Answer: ___ x ___ = ___

8.

Answer: ___ x ___ = ___

MYSTERY MESSAGE
WITH MULTIPLICATION AND DIVISION

Multiply or divide. Then use the letters to fill in the blanks below and reveal the answer to Alex's riddle.

1. $20 \div 2 =$ _____ **S**

2. $9 \times 3 =$ _____ **O**

3. $15 \div 5 =$ _____ **A**

4. $6 \times 6 =$ _____ **G**

5. $18 \div 3 =$ _____ **E**

6. $5 \times 5 =$ _____ **N**

7. $35 \div 5 =$ _____ **L**

8. $8 \times 6 =$ _____ **W**

9. $90 \div 10 =$ _____ **M**

Q: It stays alive only if it stays cold. What is it?

Copy the letters from the answers above to solve the riddle.

____ ____ ____ ____ ____ ____ ____ ____ ____ ____
 3   10   25   27   48   36   27   7   6   9

ENDERMAN'S GUIDE TO PLACE VALUE

Write the correct digit in the place value box.
The first one is done for you.

1.

726

ONES
6

2.

482

HUNDREDS

3.

629

TENS

4.

964

TENS

5.

371

HUNDREDS

6.
683

ONES

7.

392

TENS

8.
164

HUNDREDS

MATH FACTS CHALLENGE

Count by 7s and fill in the empty spaces to help Alex craft a clock with the right ingredients.

7   _____   _____   _____   28   _____   _____   _____   56   _____   70

WORD PROBLEMS WITH MULTIPLICATION

Read the word problems. Use multiplication to find the answer.

Example: You mine 3 iron ore blocks every day for 3 days. How many blocks do you mine in all?

$$3 \times 3 = 9$$

Answer: ___9 blocks___

1. There are 4 endermen and each one drops 5 ender pearls. How many ender pearls are dropped in all?

___ × ___ = ___

Answer: _____

2. There are 5 players and they each grow 6 melons in their gardens. How many melons do they grow all together?

___ × ___ = ___

Answer: _____

3. There are 7 turtles and they each spawn 3 turtle eggs. How many turtle eggs do they spawn in all?

___ × ___ = ___

Answer: _____

4. There are 8 mine shafts and they each have 2 trap doors hidden in them. How many trap doors are there in all?

___ × ___ = ___

Answer: _____

WORD PROBLEMS WITH DIVISION

Read the word problems. Use division to find the answer.

Example: The village librarian offered to give 18 of his books to Alex and Steve. They each got the same number of books. How many books did each player get?

$$18 \div 2 = 9$$

Answer: __9 books__

1. You need 20 lava blocks to build a lava field. How many lava blocks does each player need if there are 5 players working together to build it?

_____ ÷ _____ = _____

Answer: _____

2. There are 4 bees in a hive that produces a total of 12 bottles of honey. If each bee produces the same amount, how much honey does each bee produce?

_____ ÷ _____ = _____

Answer: _____

3. Alex has 24 carrots and 3 pigs to tame. How many carrots can each pig get?

_____ ÷ _____ = _____

Answer: _____

4. There are 15 torches and 3 mine shafts. How many torches can be placed in each mine shaft?

_____ ÷ _____ = _____

Answer: _____

REGROUPING IN BASE 10: MULTIPLICATION

Multiply the numbers. Then fill in the place value chart. The first one is done for you.

1. $6 \times 7 =$ __42__

Tens	Ones
4	2

2. $8 \times 8 =$ _____

Tens	Ones

3. $8 \times 4 =$ _____

Tens	Ones

4. $5 \times 8 =$ _____

Tens	Ones

5. $5 \times 6 =$ _____

Tens	Ones

6. $6 \times 8 =$ _____

Tens	Ones

7. $6 \times 4 =$ _____

Tens	Ones

8. $7 \times 3 =$ _____

Tens	Ones

REGROUPING IN BASE 10: DIVISION

Divide the numbers. Then fill in the place value chart.
The first one is done for you.

1. $20 \div 2 =$ __10__

Tens	Ones
1	0

2. $81 \div 9 =$ _____

Tens	Ones

3. $33 \div 3 =$ _____

Tens	Ones

4. $15 \div 1 =$ _____

Tens	Ones

5. $20 \div 4 =$ _____

Tens	Ones

6. $28 \div 2 =$ _____

Tens	Ones

7. $50 \div 2 =$ _____

Tens	Ones

8. $36 \div 6 =$ _____

Tens	Ones

MULTIPLICATION MATH FACTS WITH 2

Multiply the numbers. Then answer the question.

1. $3 \times 2 = $ _____

2. $5 \times 2 = $ _____

3. $7 \times 2 = $ _____

4. $10 \times 2 = $ _____

5. $8 \times 2 = $ _____

6. $9 \times 2 = $ _____

7. $11 \times 2 = $ _____

8. $6 \times 2 = $ _____

9. $12 \times 2 = $ _____

10. $2 \times 2 = $ _____

11. $2 \times 3 = $ _____

12. $2 \times 8 = $ _____

13. $2 \times 7 = $ _____

14. $11 \times 2 = $ _____

15. $2 \times 5 = $ _____

Q: Circle all of the products that are even numbers. What do you notice when you multiply a number by 2?

A:

_____

MULTIPLICATION MATH FACTS WITH 5

Multiply the numbers. Then answer the questions.

1. 3 × 5 = _____

2. 8 × 5 = _____

3. 7 × 5 = _____

4. 10 × 5 = _____

5. 9 × 5 = _____

6. 6 × 5 = _____

7. 11 × 5 = _____

8. 4 × 5 = _____

9. 1 × 5 = _____

10. 2 × 5 = _____

11. 5 × 3 = _____

12. 5 × 8 = _____

13. 5 × 7 = _____

14. 5 × 11 = _____

15. 5 × 5 = _____

Q: Circle all of the products that end in 5. What do you notice when you multiply an odd number by 5?

A: _____

Q: Put a square around all of the products that end in 0. What do you notice when you multiply an even number by 5?

A: _____

BABY ZOMBIE'S GUIDE TO PLACE VALUE

Use the number on each baby zombie to fill in the place value chart.

Example:

645

Hundreds	
6	
Tens	**Ones**
4	5

1.

342

Hundreds	
Tens	**Ones**

2.

780

Hundreds	
Tens	**Ones**

3.

912

Hundreds	
Tens	**Ones**

4.

805

Hundreds	
Tens	**Ones**

5.

926

Hundreds	
Tens	**Ones**

6.

459

Hundreds	
Tens	**Ones**

7.

603

Hundreds	
Tens	**Ones**

8.

167

Hundreds	
Tens	**Ones**

MATH FACTS CHALLENGE

Count by 8s and fill in the empty spaces to help Steve get his shield before the blaze hits him with fireballs.

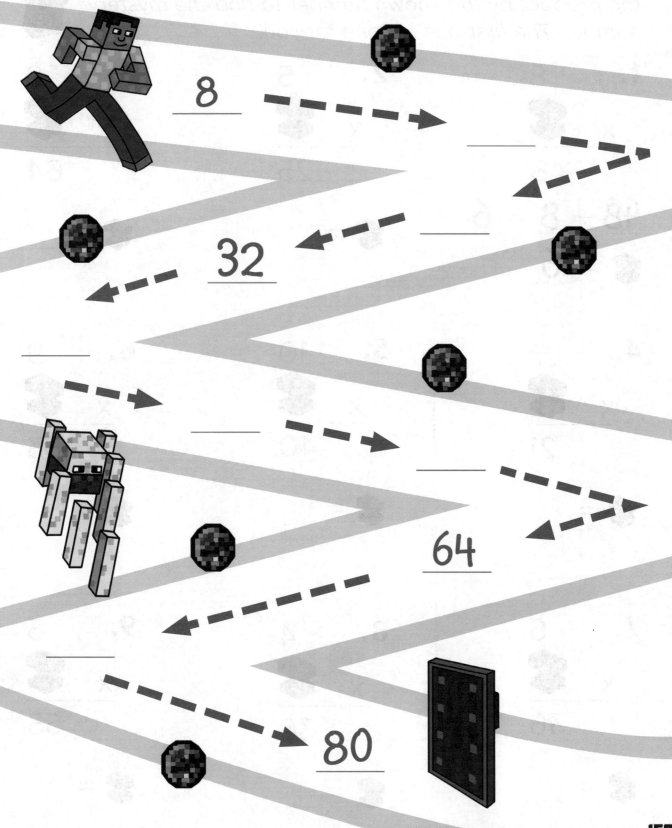

8

32

64

80

MULTIPLICATION AND DIVISION
MYSTERY NUMBER

There is a number hidden behind these anvils. Divide the product by the known number to find the mystery number. The first one is done for you.

1.
$$\begin{array}{r} 8 \\ \times \quad \blacksquare \\ \hline 48 \end{array}$$

$$\underline{48} \div \underline{8} = \underline{6}$$

$\blacksquare = 6$

2.
$$\begin{array}{r} 5 \\ \times \quad \blacksquare \\ \hline 25 \end{array}$$

$\blacksquare = \underline{\quad}$

3.
$$\begin{array}{r} 8 \\ \times \quad \blacksquare \\ \hline 64 \end{array}$$

$\blacksquare = \underline{\quad}$

4.
$$\begin{array}{r} 7 \\ \times \quad \blacksquare \\ \hline 21 \end{array}$$

$\blacksquare = \underline{\quad}$

5.
$$\begin{array}{r} 10 \\ \times \quad \blacksquare \\ \hline 40 \end{array}$$

$\blacksquare = \underline{\quad}$

6.
$$\begin{array}{r} 9 \\ \times \quad \blacksquare \\ \hline 63 \end{array}$$

$\blacksquare = \underline{\quad}$

7.
$$\begin{array}{r} 6 \\ \times \quad \blacksquare \\ \hline 36 \end{array}$$

$\blacksquare = \underline{\quad}$

8.
$$\begin{array}{r} 4 \\ \times \quad \blacksquare \\ \hline 36 \end{array}$$

$\blacksquare = \underline{\quad}$

9.
$$\begin{array}{r} 5 \\ \times \quad \blacksquare \\ \hline 55 \end{array}$$

$\blacksquare = \underline{\quad}$

MYSTERY MESSAGE
WITH MULTIPLICATION AND DIVISION

Use answers 1-8 from page 32 to fill in the chart. Then use the letters to fill in the answer and solve the riddle.

QUESTION	ANSWER	LETTER
1.		M
2.		A
3.		S
4.		L
5.		C
6.		I
7.		U
8.		E

Q: What has six faces and is very bouncy?

Copy the letters from the chart to solve the riddle.

___ ___ ___ ___ ___ ___
5   8   3   7   6   9

MULTIPLICATION IN BASE 10

Multiply the numbers. Then draw a line to the correct place value description. The first one is done for you.

1. 7 × 5 = __35__

2. 8 × 3 = ____

3. 4 × 5 = ____

4. 5 × 9 = ____

5. 7 × 9 = ____

6. 7 × 8 = ____

7. 4 × 3 = ____

8. 7 × 3 = ____

ONES
0

TENS
3

TENS
6

ONES
4

TENS
5

ONES
1

TENS
4

ONES
2

DIVISION IN BASE 10

Divide the numbers. Then draw a line to the correct place value description. The first one is done for you.

1. $27 \div 9 =$ ___3___

2. $45 \div 5 =$ _____

3. $60 \div 2 =$ _____

4. $80 \div 2 =$ _____

5. $56 \div 7 =$ _____

6. $10 \div 1 =$ _____

7. $24 \div 6 =$ _____

8. $40 \div 8 =$ _____

ONES
9

TENS
4

TENS
1

ONES
3

ONES
5

ONES
8

TENS
3

ONES
4

MULTIPLICATION MATH FACTS

Multiply the numbers. Draw a line from column A to the same answer in column B. Then answer the question. The first one is done for you.

A

1. 3 × 9 = 27
2. 5 × 6 = ___
3. 7 × 9 = ___
4. 10 × 4 = ___
5. 6 × 4 = ___
6. 9 × 2 = ___
7. 11 × 3 = ___
8. 6 × 2 = ___

B

9. 9 × 7 = ___
10. 4 × 6 = ___
11. 3 × 11 = ___
12. 6 × 5 = ___
13. 9 × 3 = 27
14. 4 × 10 = ___
15. 2 × 6 = ___
16. 2 × 9 = ___

Q: What do you notice about the order of numbers in a multiplication problem?

A: _____

MULTIPLICATION BY GROUPING

Write the multiplication sentence that matches the picture.
Then solve the equation. The first one is done for you.

1.

Answer: ___6___ x ___2___ = ___12___

2.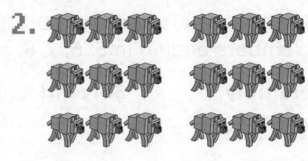

Answer: _____ x _____ = _____

3.

Answer: _____ x _____ = _____

4.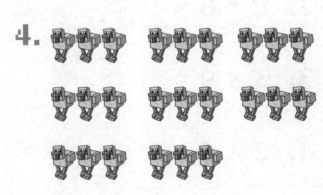

Answer: _____ x _____ = _____

5.

Answer: _____ x _____ = _____

6.

Answer: _____ x _____ = _____

7.

Answer: _____ x _____ = _____

8.

Answer: _____ x _____ = _____

ROUNDING IN BASE 10

Multiply the numbers. Then round the number up or down to the nearest ten. The first one is done for you.

Hint: Numbers ending in 0, 1, 2, 3, and 4 round *down*. Numbers ending in 5, 6, 7, 8, and 9 round *up*.

Multiply	**Solve it!**	**Round it!**
1. $6 \times 6 =$	_____	_____
2. $8 \times 6 =$	_____	_____
3. $3 \times 9 =$	_____	_____
4. $2 \times 6 =$	_____	_____
5. $7 \times 2 =$	_____	_____
6. $5 \times 7 =$	_____	_____
7. $10 \times 2 =$	_____	_____
8. $9 \times 4 =$	_____	_____
9. $4 \times 7 =$	_____	_____
10. $5 \times 4 =$	_____	_____

MATH FACTS CHALLENGE

Find the pattern and fill in the empty spaces to help Alex escape the teleporting Enderman.

9

36

72

90

WORD PROBLEMS WITH MULTIPLICATION

Read the word problems. Use multiplication to find the answer.

Example: Steve plants 4 rows of 6 potatoes. How many potatoes does Steve plant in all?

$$4 \times 6 = 24$$

Answer: **24 potatoes**

1. Alex crafts 5 diamond swords each day for a week. How many diamond swords does she have at the end of 7 days?

____ × ____ = ____

Answer: _____

2. A mob blows up 6 pigs every time it explodes. How many pigs blow up when 4 mobs explode?

____ × ____ = ____

Answer: _____

3. You need 4 blocks of wood to make one plank. How blocks of wood do you need to make 7 planks?

____ × ____ = ____

Answer: _____

4. Alex needs 3 TNT blocks to blow up each silverfish block. How many TNT blocks does she need to destroy 6 silverfish blocks?

____ × ____ = ____

Answer: _____

WORD PROBLEMS WITH DIVISION

Read the word problems. Use division to find the answer.

Example: Steve has 27 stone blocks. Each wall needs 9 stone blocks. How many walls can Steve build?

$$27 \div 9 = 3$$

Answer: __3 walls__

1. The librarian has 30 books and each shelf hold 6 books. How many shelves does the librarian need for all the books?

___ ÷ ___ = ___

Answer: _____

2. Alex collects 40 apples from 4 trees. If each tree had the same amount of apples, how many apples came from each tree?

___ ÷ ___ = ___

Answer: _____

3. Alex and Steve find a stash of 18 arrows. How many arrows can they have if they split them evenly?

___ ÷ ___ = ___

Answer: _____

4. Steve has 24 buckets of water and 6 rows of plants. How many buckets of water can he pour on each row of plants?

___ ÷ ___ = ___

Answer: _____

EXPANDED FORM IN BASE 10

Write the number on each shulker in expanded form in the space provided.

Example: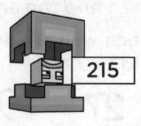
215

Answer:

200 + 10 + 5

1.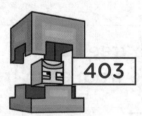
391

_____

2.
756

_____

3.
403

_____

4.
186

_____

5.
329

_____

6.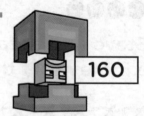
160

_____

7.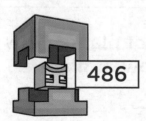
486

_____

8.
329

_____

EXPANDED FORM IN BASE 10

Write the number on each Enderman in expanded form in the space provided.

Example:
2,156

Answer:

2,000 + 100 + 50 + 6

1.
3,214

2.
1,849

3.
6,704

4.
5,096

5.
9,132

6.
4,810

7.
3,021

8.
9,305

MULTIPLICATION MATH FACTS WITH 9

Multiply the numbers.

1. $3 \times 9 =$ _____

2. $5 \times 9 =$ _____

3. $7 \times 9 =$ _____

4. $8 \times 9 =$ _____

5. $4 \times 9 =$ _____

6. $9 \times 1 =$ _____

7. $9 \times 2 =$ _____

8. $6 \times 9 =$ _____

9. $4 \times 9 =$ _____

10. $9 \times 3 =$ _____

11. $9 \times 6 =$ _____

12. $1 \times 9 =$ _____

13. $9 \times 4 =$ _____

14. $9 \times 9 =$ _____

15. $9 \times 2 =$ _____

MYSTERY MESSAGE WITH DIVISION

Divide. Then use the letters to fill in the blanks below and reveal the answer to Steve's riddle.

1. 81 ÷ 9 = _____ M

2. 42 ÷ 7 = _____ T

3. 50 ÷ 10 = _____ A

4. 36 ÷ 9 = _____ O

5. 24 ÷ 3 = _____ I

6. 80 ÷ 8 = _____ G

7. 49 ÷ 7 = _____ E

8. 18 ÷ 6 = _____ R

9. 99 ÷ 9 = _____ V

Q: How do you get a mob to scare itself?

Copy the letters from the answers above to solve the riddle.

___ ___ ___ ___   ___ ___   ___
10   8   11   7   8   6   5

___ ___ ___ ___ ___ ___
 9   8   3   3   4   3

SNOW GOLEM'S GUIDE TO PLACE VALUE

Use the chart on the right to write the number on the snow golem.

Example:

145

Hundreds	
1	
Tens	**Ones**
4	5

1.

Hundreds	
6	
Tens	**Ones**
9	4

2.

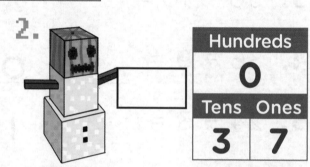

Hundreds	
0	
Tens	**Ones**
3	7

3.

Hundreds	
2	
Tens	**Ones**
0	1

4.

Hundreds	
8	
Tens	**Ones**
3	0

5.

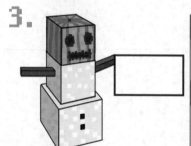

Hundreds	
4	
Tens	**Ones**
2	9

6.

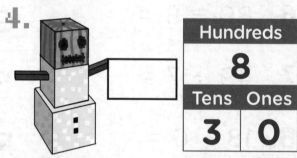

Hundreds	
5	
Tens	**Ones**
0	4

7.

Hundreds	
6	
Tens	**Ones**
7	0

8.

Hundreds	
9	
Tens	**Ones**
3	4

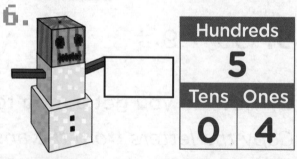

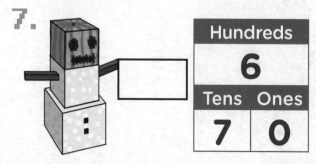

MATH FACTS CHALLENGE

Count by 4s and fill in the empty spaces to help Steve craft his diamond armor.

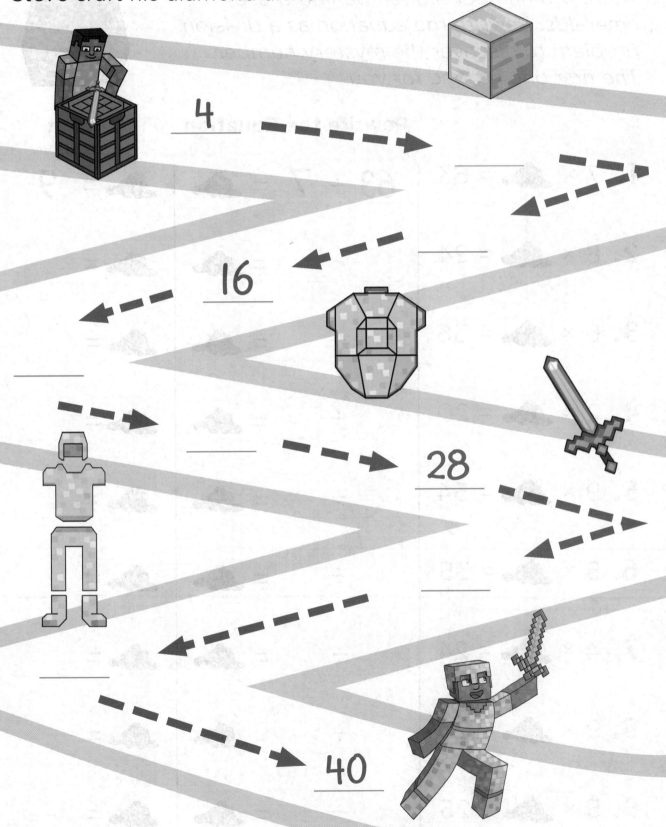

4

16

28

40

MULTIPLICATION AND DIVISION

MYSTERY NUMBER

There is a number hidden behind these emeralds. Rewrite the equation as a division problem to discover the mystery number. The first one is done for you.

	Rewrite the Equation	Solve It
1. 7 × ___ = 63	63 ÷ 7 = ___	___ = 9
2. 8 × ___ = 24	___ ÷ ___ = ___	___ = ___
3. 6 × ___ = 36	___ ÷ ___ = ___	___ = ___
4. 2 × ___ = 20	___ ÷ ___ = ___	___ = ___
5. 9 × ___ = 54	___ ÷ ___ = ___	___ = ___
6. 5 × ___ = 35	___ ÷ ___ = ___	___ = ___
7. 4 × ___ = 24	___ ÷ ___ = ___	___ = ___
8. 9 × ___ = 27	___ ÷ ___ = ___	___ = ___
9. 5 × ___ = 25	___ ÷ ___ = ___	___ = ___

MULTIPLICATION AND DIVISION
MYSTERY NUMBER

There is a number hidden behind these experience orbs. Rewrite the equation as a multiplication problem to discover the mystery number. The first one is done for you.

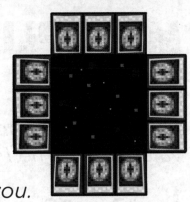

	Rewrite the Equation	**Solve It**
1. ⬡ ÷ 3 = 6	6 × 3 = ⬡	⬡ = 18
2. ⬡ ÷ 7 = 8	___ × ___ = ⬡	⬡ = ___
3. ⬡ ÷ 5 = 6	___ × ___ = ⬡	⬡ = ___
4. ⬡ ÷ 10 = 4	___ × ___ = ⬡	⬡ = ___
5. ⬡ ÷ 5 = 9	___ × ___ = ⬡	⬡ = ___
6. ⬡ ÷ 4 = 6	___ × ___ = ⬡	⬡ = ___
7. ⬡ ÷ 8 = 8	___ × ___ = ⬡	⬡ = ___
8. ⬡ ÷ 10 = 5	___ × ___ = ⬡	⬡ = ___
9. ⬡ ÷ 3 = 9	___ × ___ = ⬡	⬡ = ___

MULTIPLICATION IN BASE 10

Multiply the numbers. Then fill in the place value chart. The first one is done for you.

1. 13 × 10 = <u>130</u>

Hundreds	Tens	Ones
1	3	0

2. 54 × 10 = _____

Hundreds	Tens	Ones

3. 43 × 10 = _____

Hundreds	Tens	Ones

4. 92 × 10 = _____

Hundreds	Tens	Ones

5. 80 × 10 = _____

Hundreds	Tens	Ones

6. 34 × 10 = _____

Hundreds	Tens	Ones

7. 26 × 10 = _____

Hundreds	Tens	Ones

8. 31 × 10 = _____

Hundreds	Tens	Ones

Q: What do you notice about how a number changes when you multiply by 10?

A: _____

DIVISION IN BASE 10

Divide the numbers. Then round the number up or down to the nearest ten. The first one is done for you.

Hint: Numbers 0, 1, 2, 3, and 4 round *down*. Numbers 5, 6, 7, 8, and 9 round *up*.

Divide	Solve it!	Round it!
1. 240 ÷ 10 =	24	20
2. 690 ÷ 10 =		
3. 430 ÷ 10 =		
4. 120 ÷ 10 =		
5. 320 ÷ 10 =		
6. 470 ÷ 10 =		
7. 270 ÷ 10 =		
8. 180 ÷ 10 =		

DIVISION BY GROUPING

The villagers want to share this pie equally. Use the image of the pie to help you answer the questions.

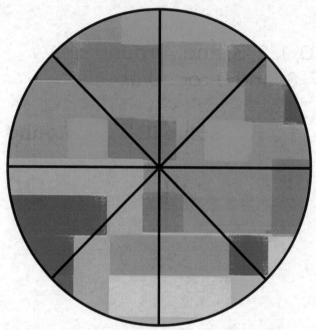

1. How many slices of this pie could 2 villagers have?

_____

2. How many slices of pie could 4 villagers have?

_____

3. How many slices of pie could 8 villagers have?

_____

4. If you wanted to feed 16 villagers, what could you do?

_____

5. If you wanted to feed 24 villagers, what could you do?

_____

MYSTERY MESSAGE
WITH MULTIPLICATION AND DIVISION

Multiply or divide. Then use the letters to fill in the blanks below and reveal the answer to Alex's riddle.

1. 72 ÷ 8 = _____ N

2. 7 × 4 = _____ U

3. 45 ÷ 9 = _____ D

4. 6 × 5 = _____ I

5. 63 ÷ 9 = _____ E

6. 8 × 4 = _____ W

7. 42 ÷ 7 = _____ O

8. 9 × 3 = _____ P

9. 56 ÷ 7 = _____ S

Q: How do you make a frowning mob smile?

Copy the letters from the answers above to solve the riddle.

T ___ ___ R ___ ___ ___ T
   28   9   30

___ ___ ___ ___ ___ ___   ___ ___ ___ ___
28 27 8 30 5 7   5 6 32 9

WITHER'S GUIDE TO PLACE VALUE

Use the chart on the right to write the number on the wither. Don't forget the comma!

Example:

Thousands	Hundreds
2	9
Tens	Ones
4	5

2,945

1.

Thousands	Hundreds
3	8
Tens	Ones
4	1

2.

Thousands	Hundreds
4	9
Tens	Ones
2	7

3.

Thousands	Hundreds
6	0
Tens	Ones
4	1

4.

Thousands	Hundreds
8	7
Tens	Ones
0	5

5.

Thousands	Hundreds
0	3
Tens	Ones
4	2

6.

Thousands	Hundreds
4	2
Tens	Ones
9	8

MATH FACTS CHALLENGE

Find the pattern and fill in the empty spaces to help Steve get to the end portal before the Ender dragon gets him.

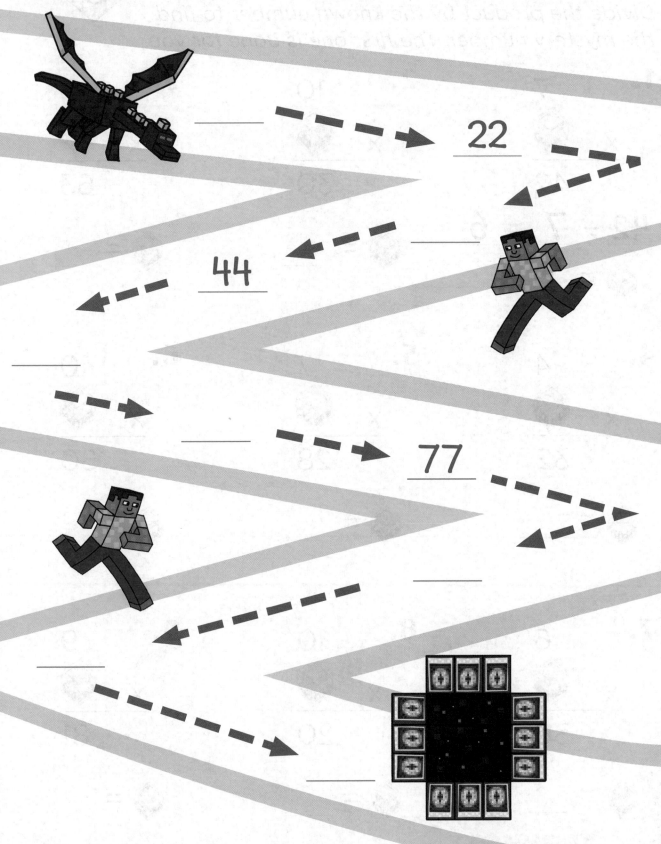

MULTIPLICATION AND DIVISION
MYSTERY NUMBER

There is a number hidden behind these beacons. Divide the product by the known number to find the mystery number. The first one is done for you.

1.
$$\begin{array}{r} 7 \\ \times \quad \square \\ \hline 42 \end{array}$$

$42 \div 7 = 6$

$\square = 6$

2.
$$\begin{array}{r} 10 \\ \times \quad \square \\ \hline 30 \end{array}$$

$\square = \underline{\quad}$

3.
$$\begin{array}{r} 9 \\ \times \quad \square \\ \hline 63 \end{array}$$

$\square = \underline{\quad}$

4.
$$\begin{array}{r} 4 \\ \times \quad \square \\ \hline 32 \end{array}$$

$\square = \underline{\quad}$

5.
$$\begin{array}{r} 7 \\ \times \quad \square \\ \hline 28 \end{array}$$

$\square = \underline{\quad}$

6.
$$\begin{array}{r} 10 \\ \times \quad \square \\ \hline 50 \end{array}$$

$\square = \underline{\quad}$

7.
$$\begin{array}{r} 6 \\ \times \quad \square \\ \hline 36 \end{array}$$

$\square = \underline{\quad}$

8.
$$\begin{array}{r} 10 \\ \times \quad \square \\ \hline 20 \end{array}$$

$\square = \underline{\quad}$

9.
$$\begin{array}{r} 9 \\ \times \quad \square \\ \hline 81 \end{array}$$

$\square = \underline{\quad}$

MYSTERY MESSAGE
WITH MULTIPLICATION AND DIVISION

Use the answers you found on page 56 to fill in the chart. Then use the letters to fill in the answer and solve the riddle.

QUESTION	ANSWER	LETTER
2.		T
3.		F
4.		O
5.		A
6.		N
7.		C
8.		I
9.		P

Q: This is a coat that will always be wet when you put it on. What is it?

___ ___ ___ ___ ___   ___ ___
4   6   8   4   3   8   7

___ ___ ___ ___ ___
9   4   2   5   3

WORD PROBLEMS WITH MULTIPLICATION

Use the information below to write a multiplication word problem. Then solve it.

Example: 4 players, 3 axes

$$\underline{\quad 4 \quad} \times \underline{\quad 3 \quad} = \underline{\quad 12 \quad}$$

Q: There are 4 players and each one has 3 swords. How many swords do they have all together?

A: They have 12 swords.

1. 5 skeletons, 6 arrows

$$\underline{\qquad} \times \underline{\qquad} = \underline{\qquad}$$

Q: _____

_____

A: _____

2. 3 ocelots, 6 fish

$$\underline{\qquad} \times \underline{\qquad} = \underline{\qquad}$$

Q: _____

_____

A: _____

3. 6 witches, 4 potions

$$\underline{\qquad} \times \underline{\qquad} = \underline{\qquad}$$

Q: _____

_____

A: _____

WORD PROBLEMS WITH DIVISION

Use the information below to write a division word problem. Then solve it.

Example: 5 fishing poles, 30 fish

$$30 \div 5 = 6$$

Q: Steve uses 5 fishing poles to catch 30 fish. If he catches the same number of fish with each pole, how many fish does each pole catch?

A: Each pole catches 6 fish.

1. 4 ender dragons, 28 dragon eggs

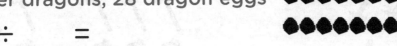

___ ÷ ___ = ___

Q: _____

_____

A: _____

2. 6 gold ingots, 18 golden swords

___ ÷ ___ = ___

Q: _____

_____

A: _____

3. 4 chickens, 12 eggs

___ ÷ ___ = ___

Q: _____

_____

A: _____

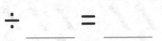

MULTIPLICATION BY GROUPING

Write the multiplication sentence that matches the picture.
Then solve the equation.

Example:

1.

Answer:

$$\underline{3} \times \underline{5} = \underline{15}$$

2. _____ × _____ = _____

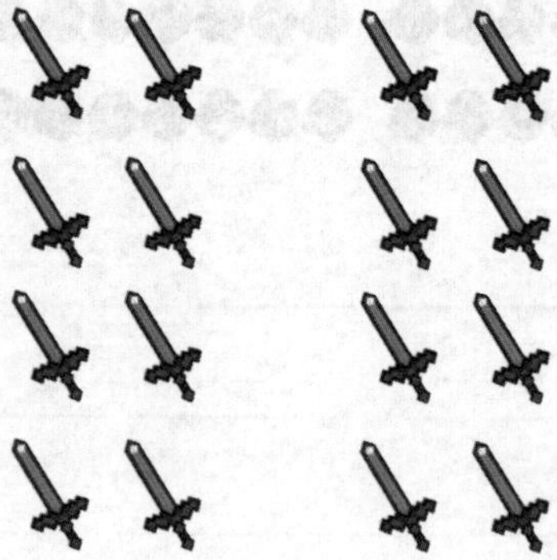

3. _____ × _____ = _____

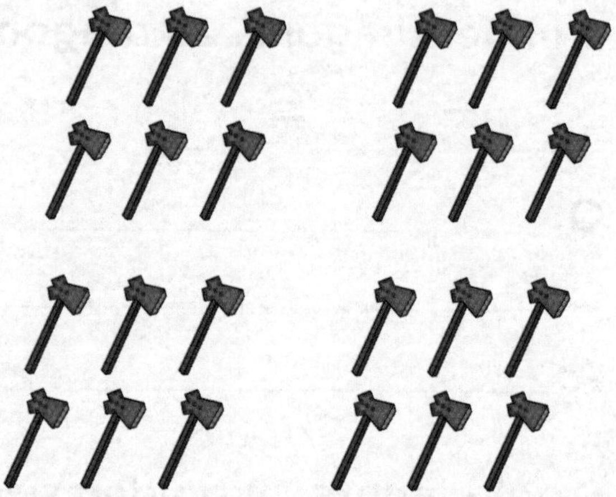

4. _____ × _____ = _____

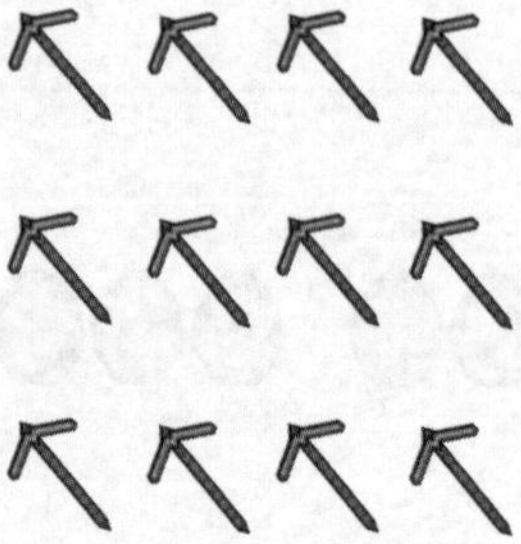

5. _____ × _____ = _____

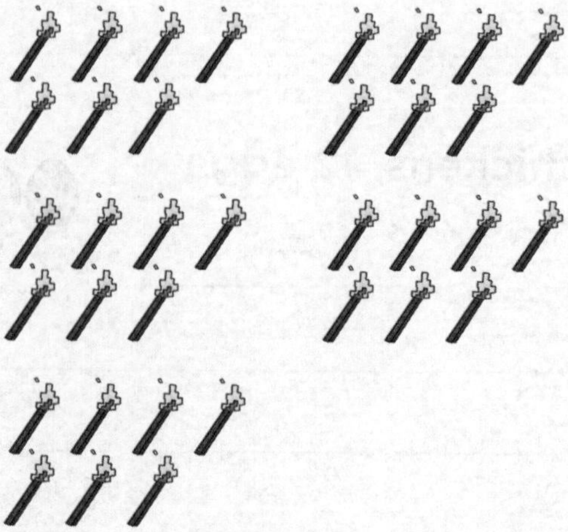

MYSTERY MESSAGE
WITH MULTIPLICATION

Multiply. Then use the letters to fill in the blanks below and reveal the answer to the joke.

1. $3 \times 8 =$ _2_4_ N   6. $7 \times 5 =$ __ __ U

2. $5 \times 6 =$ __ __ H   7. $9 \times 2 =$ __ __ O

3. $6 \times 7 =$ __ __ D   8. $8 \times 6 =$ __ __ G

4. $9 \times 8 =$ __ __ E   9. $10 \times 4 =$ __ __ R

5. $7 \times 8 =$ __ __ T

Q: What's the hardest part about falling off of a high tower?

COPY THE LETTERS FROM THE ANSWERS ABOVE TO FIND OUT.

$\overline{56}$ $\overline{30}$ $\overline{72}$

$\overline{48}$ $\overline{40}$ $\overline{18}$ $\overline{35}$ $\overset{\text{N}}{\overline{24}}$ $\overline{42}$

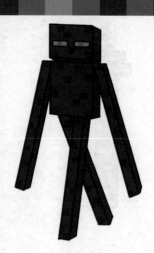

ENDERMAN'S GUIDE TO PLACE VALUE

Write the number on each Enderman in expanded form in the space provided.

Example:

1.

2,763

Answer:

2,000 + 700 + 60 + 3

2.

1,509

_____

3.

8,034

_____

4.
1,509

5,612

_____

5.

2,913

_____

6.

7,389

_____

7.

3,490

_____

MATH FACTS CHALLENGE

Find the pattern and fill in the empty spaces to help Steve escape the zombified piglin.

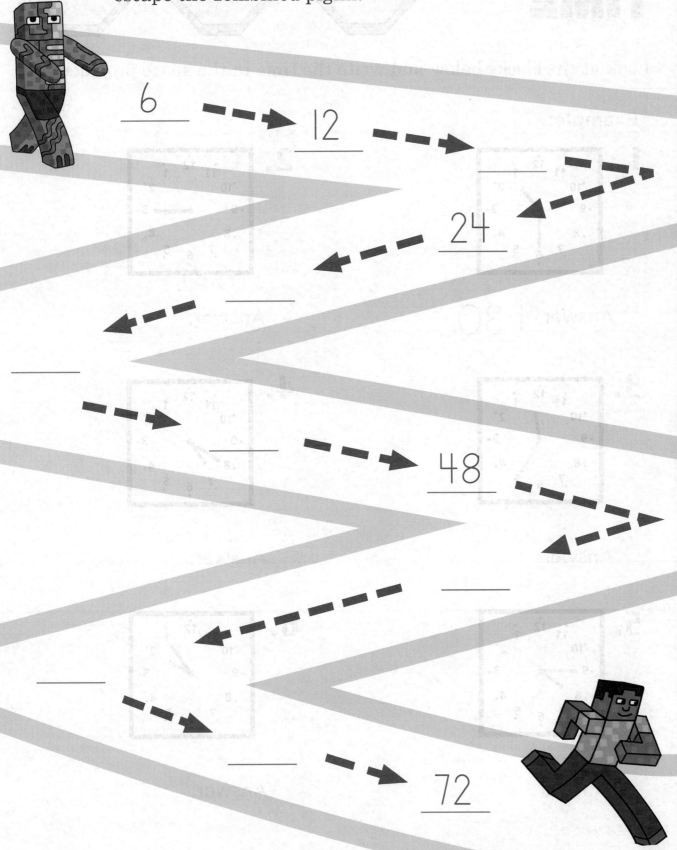

6 → 12 → ___ → 24 → ___ → ___ → ___ → 48 → ___ → ___ → ___ → ___ → 72

TELLING TIME

Look at the clocks below and write the time in the space provided:

Example:

1.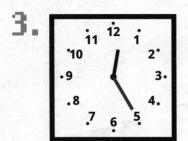

   Answer: 1:30

2.

   Answer: _____

3.

   Answer: _____

4.

   Answer: _____

5.

   Answer: _____

6.

   Answer: _____

THE TRADING TABLE

The villagers have emeralds to give Alex in exchange for her food items. Look at the table below to solve the problems that follow.

FISHERMAN	🟢	🟢					
SHEPHERD	🟢	🟢	🟢	🟢	🟢		
TOOL SMITH	🟢	🟢	🟢	🟢			
CLERIC	🟢	🟢	🟢	🟢	🟢	🟢	

Write the amount of emeralds next to each villager using the table above.

1 pile of emeralds = 7 emeralds.

1. The **fisherman** villager has _____ .

2. The **shepherd** villager has _____ .

3. The **tool smith** villager has _____ .

4. The **cleric** villager has _____ .

5. Which villagers have more emeralds than the **tool smith** villager? _____

6. Which villager has the least amount of emeralds? _____

7. The **fisherman** wants to have as many emeralds as the **cleric**. Which villager's collection does she need to add to hers? _____

GEOMETRY SKILLS PRACTICE

How many items are in each array? Count the number of items in one row and one column. Write a multiplication sentence to find the answer.

Example:

1. $\underline{2}$ x $\underline{4}$ = $\underline{8}$

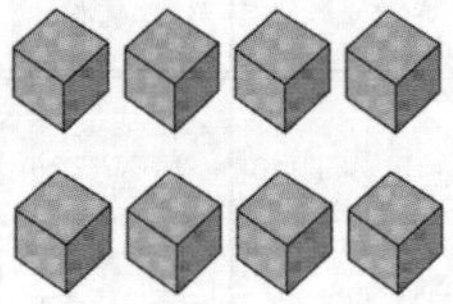

2. ___ x ___ = ___

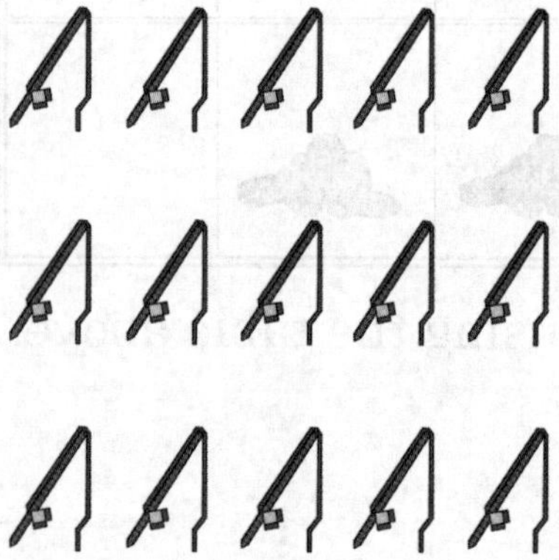

3. ___ x ___ = ___

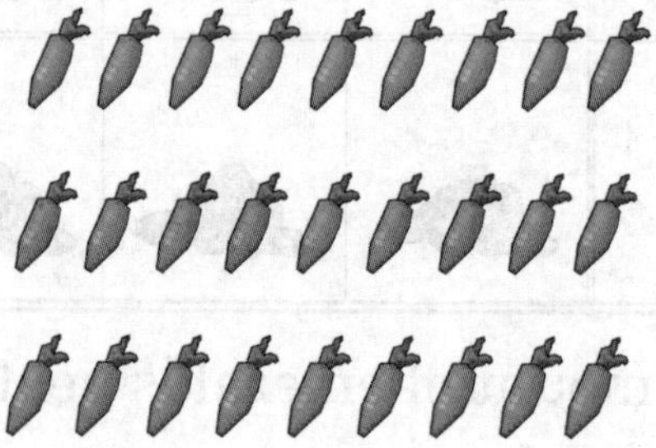

4. ___ x ___ = ___

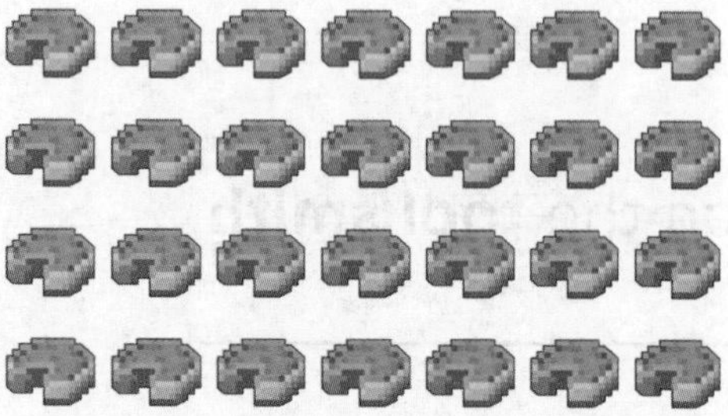

5. ___ x ___ = ___

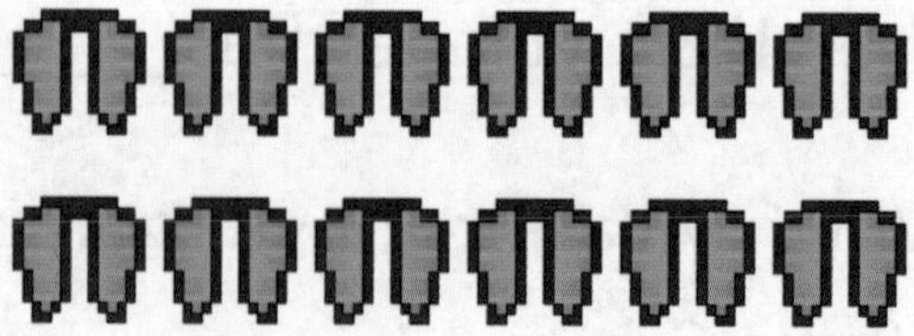

6. _____ x _____ = _____

7. _____ x _____ = _____

8. _____ x _____ = _____

9. _____ x _____ = _____

HARDCORE MODE: Try this hardcore math challenge!

_____ x _____ = _____ + _____ = _____

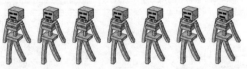
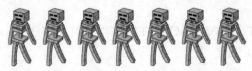

MULTIPLICATION WORD PROBLEMS

Read the problem carefully. Draw a picture or write a number sentence to help you solve the problem.

Example:

1. A zombie villager needs to be fed 2 golden apples to turn back into a villager. How many apples do you need to cure 3 zombie villagers?

Answer: <u>6 golden apples</u>

$$3 \times 2 = 6$$

2. You need 8 diamonds to make 1 chestplate. How many diamonds do you need to make 2 chestplates?

Answer: _____

3. You need 4 grass blocks to make a path along 1 side of your square house. How many grass blocks do you need to make a path on 4 sides of your house?

Answer: _____

4. A cow gives 3 buckets of milk per day. How many buckets of milk will you have after 7 days?

Answer: _____

5. A chicken lays 4 eggs a day. How many eggs will you have at the end of the day if your farm has 5 chickens?

Answer: _____

6. You need 9 wood blocks to make 1 large crafting table. How many wood blocks do you need to make 3 large crafting tables?

Answer: _____

7. A total of 3 TNT blocks will destroy 1 skeleton. How many TNT blocks do you need to destroy 5 skeletons?

Answer: _____

8. Alex uses 1 carrot to tame 1 pig. How many carrots will she need to tame 7 pigs?

Answer: _____

9. You need 3 blocks of snow to make 1 snow golem. How many blocks of snow do you need to make 6 snow golems?

Answer: _____

SNOW GOLEM'S GUIDE TO PLACE VALUE

Answer the multiplication questions below.
Then round to the closest ten.

Solve It!   **Round It!**

1. 2 x 4 =   8   10

2. 6 x 4 = ___   ___

3. 3 x 3 = ___   ___

4. 7 x 7 = ___   ___

5. 9 x 8 = ___   ___

6. 8 x 7 = ___   ___

7. 5 x 6 = ___   ___

MATH FACTS CHALLENGE

Count by 3 and practice your math facts to help the ocelot get the fish.

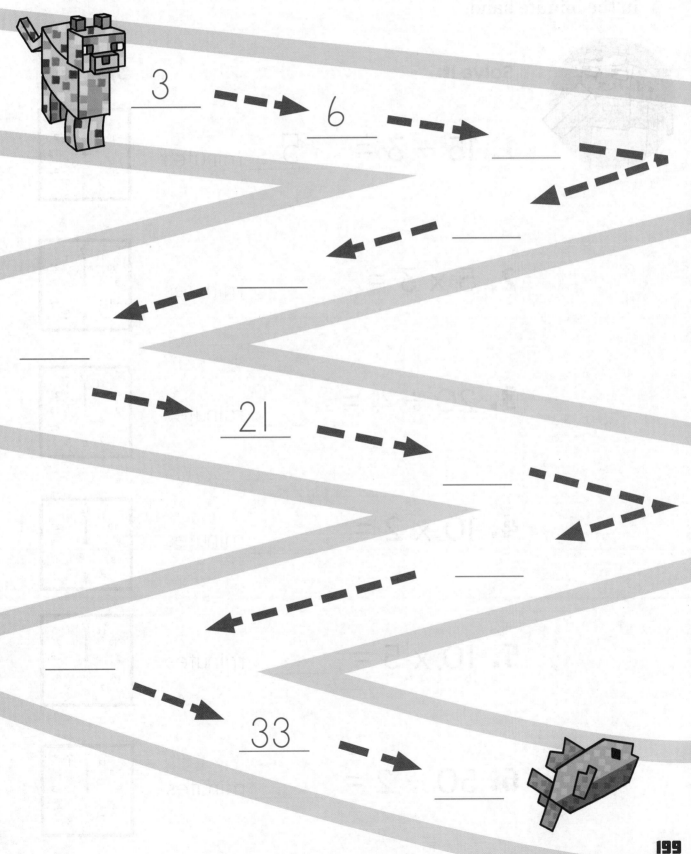

3 ⟶ 6 ⟶ ___ ⟶ ___ ⟶ ___ ⟶ 21 ⟶ ___ ⟶ ___ ⟶ ___ ⟶ 33 ⟶ ___

MINUTE HAND MYSTERY

A computer glitch erased the minute hands from these clocks! Solve the problem to find out how many minutes have passed, then draw in the minute hand.

Solve it.

Draw it.

1. $15 \div 3 =$ ___5___ minutes

2. $5 \times 3 =$ _____ minutes

3. $20 \div 4 =$ _____ minutes

4. $10 \times 2 =$ _____ minutes

5. $10 \times 5 =$ _____ minutes

6. $50 \div 2 =$ _____ minutes

EQUAL TRADE

This librarian villager loves trading for new coins. Figure out the right number of coins to trade so that you don't lose any money in the deal.

1. How many **nickels** equal 1 dime?

Answer: _____

2. How many **pennies** equal 1 quarter?

Answer: _____

3. How many **nickels** equal 2 dimes?

Answer: _____

4. How many **dimes** equal a dollar?

Answer: _____

5. How many **pennies** equal 2 quarters?

Answer: _____

ADVENTURES IN GEOMETRY

Which of these gaming images are symmetrical? Circle the number.

Symmetrical = an object that can be divided with a line into two matching halves.

1.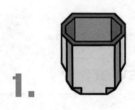

2.

3.

4.

5.

6.

CREATIVE MODE
Complete the other half of this drawing to make it as symmetrical as possible:

SHELTER GEOMETRY

Alex and Steve have been working all afternoon to build a new shelter out of redstone blocks.

Area=
height x width

1. Calculate the area of Alex's wall:

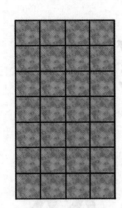

_____ x _____ = _____

2. Calculate the area of Steve's wall:

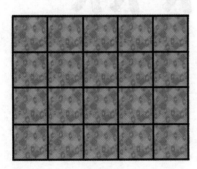

_____ x _____ = _____

3. Which player's wall has the greatest area? _____

4. How many more blocks did that player use? _____

5. If you combine their two walls, what would the area of their new, larger wall be? _____

MULTIPLICATION BY GROUPING

Count each group of 4, then finish the equation to find the answer.

1.  _____ × 4 = _____

2. _____ × 4 = _____

3.  _____ × 4 = _____

4. _____ × 4 = _____

5. _____ × 4 = _____

MYSTERY MESSAGE
WITH MULTIPLICATION AND DIVISION

Solve the problems below to find out which number matches with which letter. Then put the correct letters into the message to answer the riddle!

1. 136 ÷ 2 = <u>68</u>   E

2. 27 x 4 = _____   O

3. 32 x 3 = _____   H

4. 623 ÷ 7 = _____   R

5. 124 x 6 = _____   B

6. 256 ÷ 8 = _____   N

7. 103 x 9 = _____   I

8. 248 ÷ 8 = _____   G

9. 62 x 6 = _____   S

Q: What do you call horses that linger near your structure?

COPY THE LETTERS FROM THE ANSWERS ABOVE TO FIND OUT.

32	68	927	31	96	744	108	89	372

GHAST'S GUIDE TO PLACE VALUE

Solve the multiplication equations below. Match each answer to the correct place value description on the right.

 1. 9 x 7 = 63   **A.** 3 hundreds

 2. 6 x 8 = ___   **B.** 3 ones

 3. 7 x 9 = ___   **C.** 4 tens

 4. 10 x 30 = ___   **D.** 3 tens

 5. 8 x 4 = ___   **E.** 6 ones

 6. 11 x 7 = ___   **F.** 6 tens

7. 6 x 6 = ___   **G.** 7 ones

SKIP COUNT CHALLENGE

You have the right light levels to grow 5 mushrooms each day. Count by 5 to find out how many mushrooms you'll have at the end of 12 days.

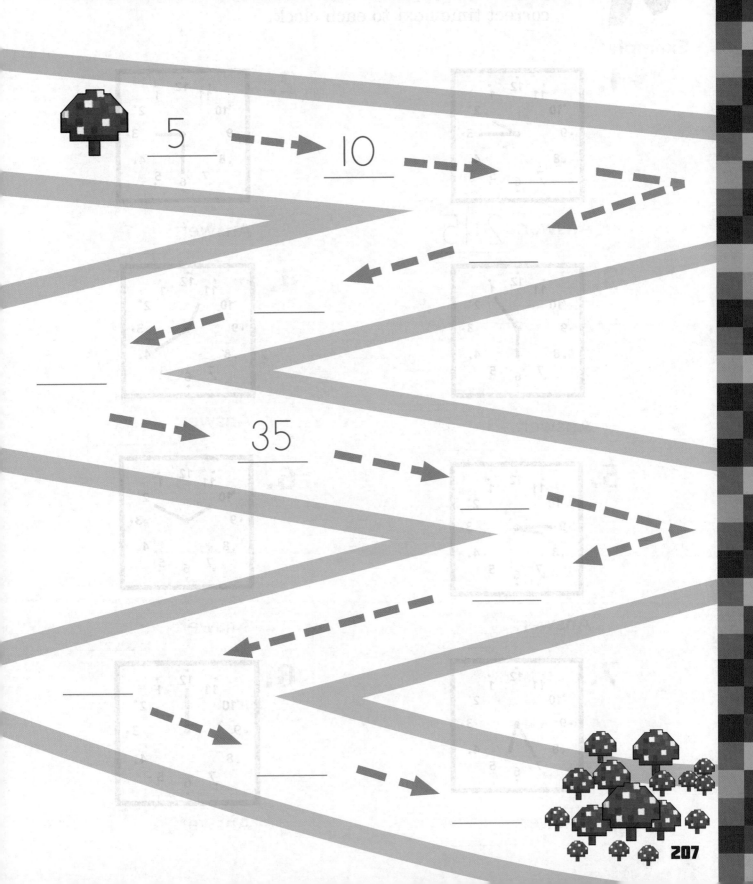

TELLING TIME

The baby zombie is learning how to tell time but needs your help. Help the baby zombie by writing down the correct time next to each clock.

Example:

1.

Answer: 2:15

2.

Answer: _____

3.

Answer: _____

4.

Answer: _____

5.

Answer: _____

6.

Answer: _____

7.

Answer: _____

8.

Answer: _____

FISH BUCKET CHALLENGE

Solve the equations next to each colored bucket to find out how many fish each one can hold.

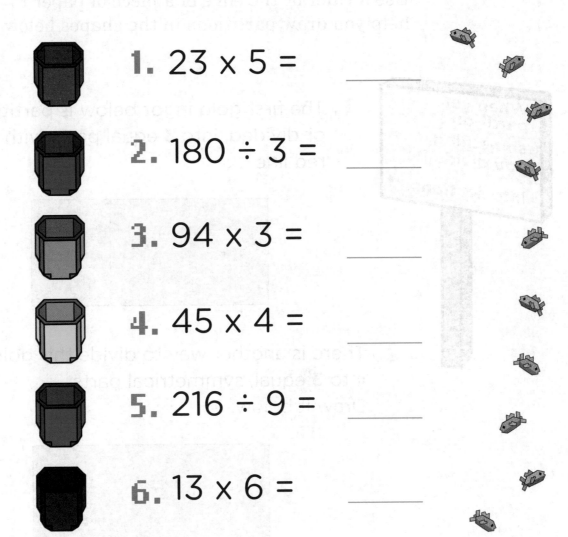

1. 23 x 5 = _____

2. 180 ÷ 3 = _____

3. 94 x 3 = _____

4. 45 x 4 = _____

5. 216 ÷ 9 = _____

6. 13 x 6 = _____

7. Which colored bucket can hold the most fish? _____

8. Which two colored buckets, when combined, add up to 102 fish? _____ and _____

HARDCORE MODE: Try this hardcore math challenge!

What is the sum of all the fish in all the buckets? _____

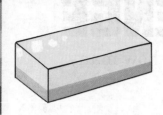

EQUAL PARTS CHALLENGE

Use a ruler or the edge of a piece of paper to help you draw partitions in the shapes below.

When you partition something, you divide it into sections

1. The first gold ingot below is partitioned, or divided, into **3** equal parts with the red line.

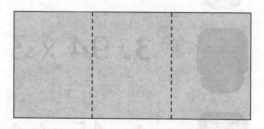

2. There is another way to divide this gold ingot into **3** equal, symmetrical parts.
Draw it below:

3. Use your pencil to shade in one of the pieces above.
What fraction describes this picture?

_____

4. Partition the iron ingot into **4** equal shares in two different ways.

Use your pencil to shade in one of the pieces above. What fraction describes this picture? _____

5. Partition the iron ingot into **6** equal shares in two different ways.

Use your pencil to shade in one of the pieces above. What fraction describes this picture? _____

MYSTERY MESSAGE WITH MULTIPLICATION

Solve each multiplication equation below. Use the answers to solve the riddle.

1. 26
×9
_____
234

U

2. 38
×7

J

3. 54
×8

Y

4. 27
×6

B

5. 42
×5

F

6. 49
×8

I

7. 19
×7

E

8. 95
×5

C

Q: Where does Steve go to get his cart serviced?

COPY THE LETTERS FROM THE ANSWERS ABOVE TO FIND OUT.

266 392 210 210 432

475 234 162 133

MULTIPLICATION AND DIVISION MYSTERY NUMBER

Some hacker has replaced a number from each of the below equations with a pufferfish. Use multiplication and division to solve for the missing numbers.

1. $3 \times$ 🐡 $= \underline{18}$ 🐡 $= \underline{6}$

2. 🐡 $\div 6 = \underline{4}$ 🐡 $= \underline{}$

3. $150 \div$ 🐡 $= \underline{15}$ 🐡 $= \underline{}$

4. $7 \times$ 🐡 $= \underline{21}$ 🐡 $= \underline{}$

5. $54 \div$ 🐡 $= \underline{9}$ 🐡 $= \underline{}$

6. 🐡 $\times 8 = \underline{72}$ 🐡 $= \underline{}$

7. $36 \div$ 🐡 $= \underline{3}$ 🐡 $= \underline{}$

8. 🐡 $\times 12 = \underline{48}$ 🐡 $= \underline{}$

9. $77 \div$ 🐡 $= \underline{7}$ 🐡 $= \underline{}$

10. $42 \div$ 🐡 $= \underline{7}$ 🐡 $= \underline{}$

ENDER DRAGON'S NUMBER CHALLENGE

Match the Ender Dragon with the description of the number.

1. Hundreds: **1** Tens: **6** Ones: **2**

A.
633÷3

2. Hundreds: **2** Tens: **1** Ones: **1**

B.
42x8

3. Hundreds: **4** Tens: **4** Ones: **8**

C.
18x9

4. Hundreds: **3** Tens: **3** Ones: **6**

D.
795÷5

5. Hundreds: **1** Tens: **5** Ones: **9**

E.
64x7

SKIP COUNT CHALLENGE

Three zombie villagers are after you. Count by 4 to find the splash potion of weakness and cure them.

4

8

60

CREATING POTIONS

Use the recipes below to figure out the number of items needed to make more of each potion.

1. = 4 awkward potions + 2 glistering melons

= _____ awkward potions +

_____ glistering melons

2. = 3 awkward potions + 6 sugars

= _____ awkward potions + _____ sugars

3. = 5 golden carrots + 8 nether warts

= _____ golden carrots +

_____ nether warts

INVISIBILITY POTION FORMULA

4. 🧪 = 3 potions of night vision + 6 fermented spider eyes

🧪🧪🧪
🧪🧪🧪🧪 = _____ potions of night vision +
_____ fermented spider eyes

INVISIBILITY POTION INGREDIENTS TABLE

Use the formula above to determine how much you need of each ingredient below. The first one is done for you.

	🧪🧪	🧪🧪🧪	🧪🧪🧪	🧪🧪🧪🧪
Night Vision Potion	6			
Fermented Spider Eyes				

217

ADVENTURES IN GEOMETRY: PERIMETER AND AREA

Alex is building new rooms in her house. Multiply the number of blocks to help her find the perimeter and area of the walls.

perimeter = 2 x height + 2 x width

1. Perimeter = ____

If Alex triples the height of this wall,

what would the new perimeter be? ____

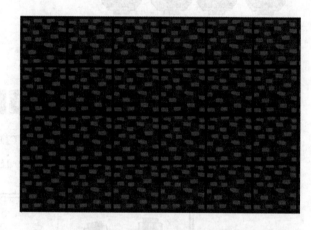

2. Perimeter = ____

If Alex destroys the right half of this wall, what would the new perimeter be? ____

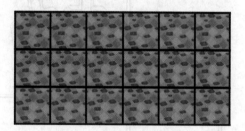

3. Perimeter = ____

Alex built a wall twice as wide as this one. What was the perimeter of her new wall?

____

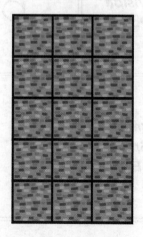

area =
height x
width

4. Area = _____

If Alex doubles the height of this wall,
what would the new area be? _____

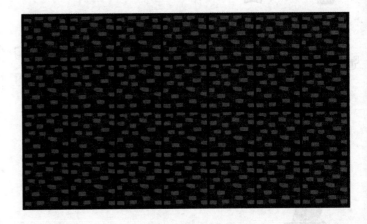

5. Area = _____

If Alex destroys the right half of this wall,
what would the new area be? _____

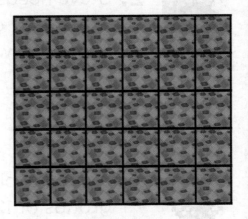

6. Area = _____

Alex built a wall twice as tall as this one.
What was the area of her wall? _____

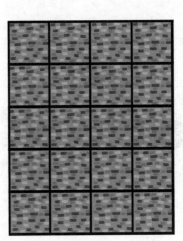

WORD PROBLEMS

Use multiplication and division to solve these word problems.

1. Alex must feed her pig 4 carrots before she can ride it. If she wants to ride her pig 7 times, how many carrots does she need?

Answer: _____

2. Steve needs 3 diamonds to craft a diamond sword. How many diamonds will he need to craft 9 diamond swords?

Answer: _____

3. As you explore the Plains biome, you pass 2 different groups of 12 flowers. How many flowers do you pass in all?

Answer: _____

4. Steve is mining for iron ore. He breaks each block into 6 pieces. In the end he has 30 pieces of ore. How many blocks did he start with?

Answer: _____

5. Each melon block drops 4 slices and each slice is cut into 3 pieces. If you have 5 melon blocks, how many melon pieces will you get?

Answer: _____

6. If Alex's bow shoots 6 enchanted arrows per hour and Steve's bow shoots 4, how many arrows total will they shoot in 8 hours?

Answer: _____

7. Alex has 3 bees. Each bee breeds 4 baby bees in one hour. How many bees does Alex have at the end of 3 hours?

Answer: _____

8. Steve and Alex lose 3 damage hearts time they battle a spider. One day, they both fight 3 spiders. How many hearts do they lose in all?

Answer: _____

PLACE VALUE

Match the answer to each equation on the left with the number of flowers on the right to help Steve calculate how many flowers he planted in total.

1. $7 \times 3 \times 8 =$ _____

2. $13 \times 8 \times 6 =$ _____

3. $14 \times 7 \times 3 =$ _____

4. $5 \times 10 \times 7 =$ _____

5. $12 \times 7 \times 5 =$ _____

6. $9 \times 11 \times 5 =$ _____

7. $26 \times 4 \times 8 =$ _____

A. 350

B. 168

C. 624

D. 495

E. 832

F. 420

G. 294

SQUID NUMBER CHALLENGE

Match the answer to the equation on the right with the correct place value description on the left.

1. Hundreds: **1** Tens: **8** Ones: **0**

2. Hundreds: **1** Tens: **0** Ones: **3**

3. Hundreds: **2** Tens: **2** Ones: **8**

4. Hundreds: **7** Tens: **3** Ones: **8**

5. Hundreds: **3** Tens: **3** Ones: **6**

6. Hundreds: **2** Tens: **9** Ones: **4**

7. Hundreds: **0** Tens: **9** Ones: **1**

A. 76 x 3

B. 82 x 9

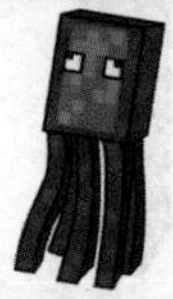

C. 14 x 21

D. 309 ÷ 3

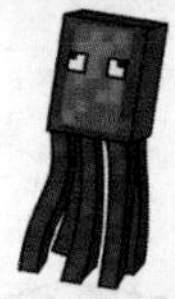

E. 546 ÷ 6

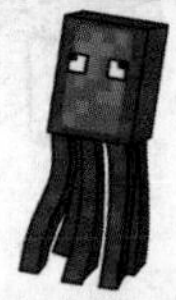

F. 36 x 5

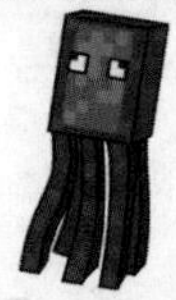

G. 42 x 8

MOB MEASUREMENTS

Use multiplication and addition to measure the height of each animal.

1 foot = 12 inches

Example:

1.

Goat
2 feet, 6 inches

12 x 2 = <u>24</u> inches

24 + 6 = <u>30</u> inches tall

2.

Pig

2 feet, 2 inches

Height in inches = _____

3.

Cow

3 feet, 5 inches

Height in inches = _____

4.

Sheep

3 feet, 8 inches

Height in inches = _____

5.

Chicken

1 foot, 9 inches

Height in inches = _____

METRIC MEASUREMENTS

Complete the chart using the formula provided.

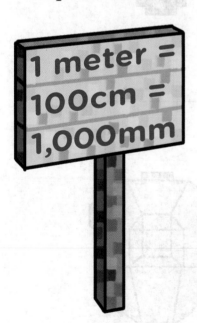

1 meter =
100cm =
1,000mm

	Length in meters	Length in cm	Length in mm
	1	100	1,000
		300	
	1.5		1,500
			2,700

ADVENTURES IN GEOMETRY

Identify the angle shown in each picture as acute, right, or obtuse.

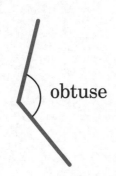 obtuse

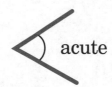 acute

 right

1. _____

2. _____

3. _____

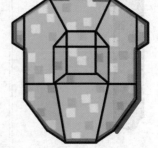

4. _____

MULTIPLICATION AND DIVISION
MYSTERY NUMBER

5. _____

6. _____

7. _____

8. _____

MULTIPLICATION AND DIVISION MYSTERY NUMBER

A troublesome griefer has replaced a number in each equation with a turtle spawn egg! Use multiplication and division to determine the missing number.

1. 248 ÷ ● = 31   ● = _____

2. ● ÷ 5 = 24   ● = _____

3. 279 ÷ 9 = ●   ● = _____

4. 636 ÷ ● = 106   ● = _____

5. 196 ÷ 7 = ●   ● = _____

6. ● ÷ 3 = 256   ● = _____

7. 72 ÷ ● = 8   ● = _____

8. 510 ÷ 6 = ●   ● = _____

9. 9 × ● = 315   ● = _____

MYSTERY MESSAGE
WITH MULTIPLICATION AND DIVISION

Solve the multiplication and division problems below. Then write the letters in the blank spaces at the bottom of the page to get the answer to the joke!

1. $624 \div 4 =$ _____ I

2. $23 \times 7 =$ _____ B

3. $612 \div 9 =$ _____ A

4. $546 \div 7 =$ _____ R

5. $39 \times 5 =$ _____ Y

6. $124 \times 3 =$ _____ L

Q: Which building has the most stories?

COPY THE LETTERS FROM THE ANSWERS ABOVE TO FIND OUT.

Answer:

____ ____ ____ ____ ____ ____ ____ ____
68   372 156 161 78   68   78   195

IRON GOLEM'S GUIDE TO PLACE VALUE

Solve the division equations below to fill in the empty place value box beside each one.

1. 801 ÷ 3 = ____

Hundreds

2. 335 ÷ 5 = ____

Ones

3. 1,404 ÷ 9 = ____

Tens

4. 672 ÷ 21 = ____

Ones

5. 480 ÷ 15 = ____

Tens

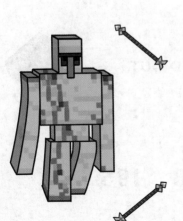

6. 2,056 ÷ 4 = ____

Hundreds

7. 406 ÷ 7 = ____

Ones

SKIP COUNT CHALLENGE

A zombie in gold armor has discovered you in the forest! Figure out the number pattern and fill in the blanks to complete the path before he can catch you.

ANIMAL TALLY

Use the six clues below to help you fill in the chart on the right-hand page.

1. If Steve can fit 5 chickens at each of his farms and he has 2 farms full of chickens, plus 3 extra chickens that he keeps in his house, how many chickens total does he have?

2. If Alex has 3 times as many chickens as Steve, how many does she have?

3. If Steve has 46 horses and Alex has ¹/₂ the amount that he has, how many horses does she have?

4. If Steve has 18 sheep and Alex has 4 times that number of sheep, how many sheep does she have?

5. If Steve has 7 groups of 12 cows, how many cows does he have?

6. If Alex has ¹/₆ the amount of cows as Steve, how many cows does she have total?

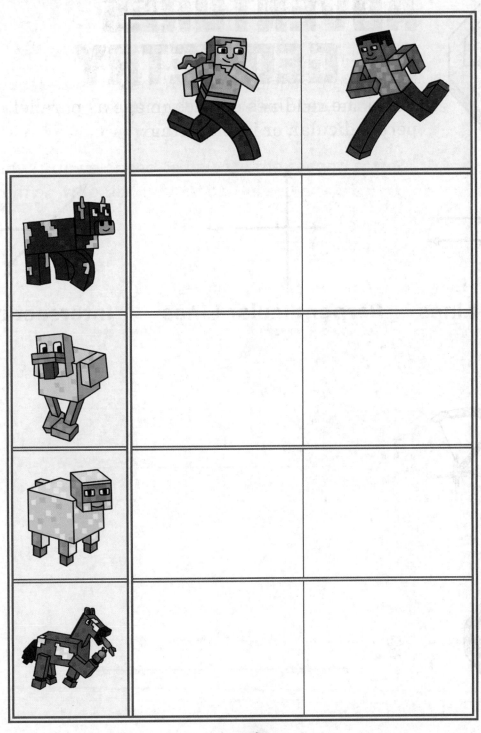

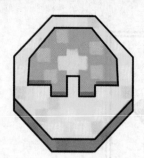

ADVENTURES IN GEOMETRY

Label the red lines on each image as parallel, perpendicular, or intersecting.

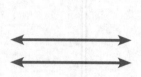

Parallel Lines

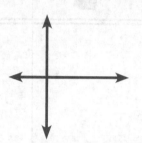

Perpendicular Lines

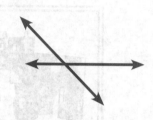

Intersecting Lines

1. _____

2. _____

3. _____

4. _____

5. _____

6. _____

7. _____

WORD PROBLEMS

Use multiplication and division to solve these word problems.

1. Alex's pig will walk 5 feet before eating the dangling carrot. Alex wants her pig to walk 250 feet. How many carrots will she need?

2. Each melon slice has 4 seeds. After Steve cuts up his melon block he has 52 seeds. How many slices were in his melon block?

3. Each shelf in the library holds 10 books. The library has 63 shelves. How many books are there in total?

4. A bee lives in a hive with 120 other bees. A mob of skeletons shake the hive and ⅓ of the bees fly away. How many bees are left?

5. A golden thread that is 6 inches long lets you cast 4 enchantments. If the thread is 54 inches long, how many enchantments can you cast?

6. A torch will light up 7 blocks. You want to get back to your house, which is 490 blocks away. How many torches will you need to light your path?

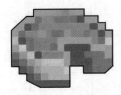

7. You made 22 pumpkin pies for your friends, and each pie will be cut into 8 slices. A wolf eats 1 slice out of every pie. How many slices do you have left for your friends?

GIANT'S GUIDE TO PLACE VALUE

Answer the multiplication and division questions below. Write the correct digit in the place value box.

1. 568 ÷ 4 =

2. 2765 ÷ 7 =

3. 19,450 ÷ 10 =

4. 456 x 12 =

5. 302,576 ÷ 8 =

6. 1045 ÷ 5 =

7. 389,724 ÷ 3 =

Tens

Hundreds

Thousands

Ones

Ten Thousands

Hundreds

Hundred Thousands

SKIP COUNT CHALLENGE

You've stumbled upon a shulker hiding in the bushes!
Find the pattern to fill in the blanks to finish the
path and get to your house.

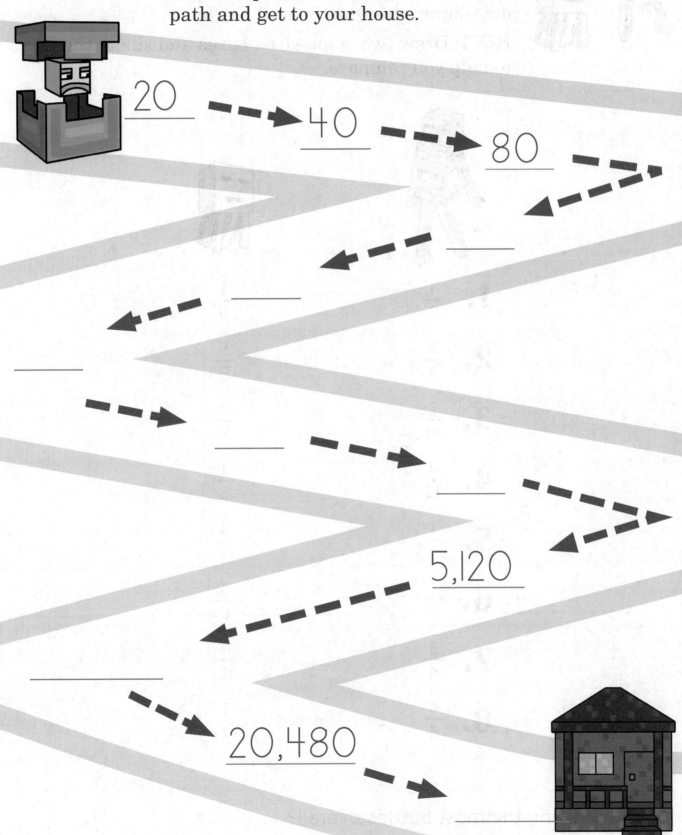

20

40

80

_____

_____

_____

_____

_____

_____

5,120

_____

20,480

_____

COMPARING FRACTIONS

Can a skeleton take down a ghast? Compare the fractions and circle the one that is greater to determine who wins in each battle.

HINT: Draw two same-sized boxes and shade them in to help you compare.

1. $\frac{1}{3}$ $\frac{1}{6}$

2. $\frac{3}{4}$ $\frac{5}{8}$

3. $\frac{2}{16}$ $\frac{2}{8}$

4. $\frac{4}{15}$ $\frac{1}{5}$

5. $\frac{1}{4}$ $\frac{4}{12}$

6. $\frac{1}{3}$ $\frac{3}{6}$

7. $\frac{3}{4}$ $\frac{11}{16}$

8. $\frac{4}{6}$ $\frac{1}{2}$

Who won the most battles overall?

_____

EQUAL FRACTIONS

One day in Steve's world is 120 minutes in real life! Use multiplication and division to fill in the chart and find out how much time Steve spends on each activity.

	Minutes out of one-fourth day (30 minutes)	Minutes out of half a day (60 minutes)	Minutes out of a day (120 minutes)
farming	$\frac{1}{30}$	$\frac{2}{60}$	$\frac{4}{120}$
fighting	$\frac{4}{30}$	$\frac{}{60}$	$\frac{}{120}$
crafting	$\frac{10}{30}$	$\frac{}{60}$	$\frac{}{120}$
mining	$\frac{}{30}$	$\frac{}{60}$	$\frac{60}{120}$

What does Steve spend most of his day doing? _____

GEOMETRY WORD PROBLEMS

Solve the problems using multiplication and division.

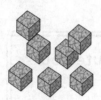

1. If Alex builds a square wall out of lapis lazuli and the wall has an area of 25 square feet, how many feet long is each side of the wall?

2. A Minecrafter's bookcase is shaped like a cube. If each side of that cube is 3 feet long, how many bookcases can you squeeze onto a 144-square-foot floor?

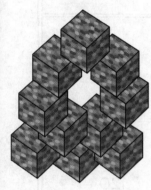

3. Alex has a rectangular fenced-in area that is 5,400 square feet. If the length of the fence is 90 feet, how wide is it?

4. Steve walks the perimeter of his house three times each day to check for zombies. If all the sides of his house are 16 feet long, how many feet does Steve walk every day?

5. Alex's treasure chest measures 10 feet by 8 feet. She can fit 4 emeralds in every square foot. How many emeralds can she fit in the chest?

6. Steve built a rectangular obsidian wall that has a perimeter of 34 feet. If the wall is 7 feet long, how wide is it?

7. Steve wants to fit all 16 of his pet cats inside his house. If each cat needs 4 square feet to move freely, how long do the sides of his square house have to be?

ANSWER KEY

Page 132

1. 8
2. 10
3. 6
4. 15

Page 133

1. 27
2. 24
3. 50
4. 42
5. 35
6. 22
7. 30
8. 72

Jiffy Cube

Page 134

1. 800 + 00 + 1
2. 100 + 60 + 7
3. 400 + 50 + 0
4. 800 + 30 + 4
5. 300 + 20 + 6
6. 700 + 30 + 5

Page 135

5, 10, 15, 20, 25, 30, 35, 40, 45, 50, 55

Page 136

1. 4
2. 5
3. 2
4. 6
5. 3
6. 0

Page 137

1. 7
2. 8
3. 6
4. 5
5. 8
6. 9

Page 138

1. 56; 5 tens 6 ones
2. 35; 3 tens, 5 ones
3. 24; 2 tens, 4 ones
4. 63; 6 tens, 3 ones
5. 64; 6 tens, 4 ones
6. 18; 1 ten, 8 ones
7. 50; 5 tens, 0 ones
8. 27; 2 tens, 7 ones

Page 139

1. 6; 10
2. 8; 10
3. 3; 0
4. 2; 0
5. 7; 10
6. 6; 10
7. 2; 0
8. 4; 0

Page 140

1. 12
2. 24
3. 15
4. 16
5. 21
6. 35

Page 141

1. 2
2. 6
3. 10
4. 5
5. 9
6. 3
7. 7
8. 4

Guardians

Page 142

1. 9
2. 6
3. 0
4. 3
5. 8
6. 5
7. 0
8. 1

Page 143

6, 12, 18, 24, 30, 36, 42, 48, 54, 60, 66

Page 144

1. 2
2. 3
3. 5
4. 3
5. 4
6. 5
7. 1
8. 2
9. 3

Page 145

1. 20
2. 9
3. 10
4. 16
5. 20
6. 12
7. 24
8. 28
9. 21

Page 146

1. 32; 3 tens, 2 ones
2. 30; 3 tens, 0 ones
3. 9; 0 tens, 9 ones
4. 24; 2 tens, 4 ones
5. 20; 2 tens, 0 ones
6. 16; 1 ten, 6 ones
7. 27; 2 tens, 7 ones
8. 36; 3 tens, 6 ones

Page 147

1. 10
2. 30
3. 60
4. 20
5. 50
6. 80
7. 90
8. 70
9. 100
10. 40

You add a 0 to the end of the number and get a two-digit number.

You add a 0 to the end of the number and get a three-digit number. Examples: 100, 200, 300

Page 148

1. 21
2. 20
3. 30
4. 24
5. 18
6. 12
7. 18
8. 15

Page 149

1. 10
2. 27
3. 3
4. 36
5. 6
6. 25
7. 7
8. 48
9. *A snow golem*

Page 150

1. 6
2. 4
3. 2
4. 6
5. 3
6. 3
7. 9
8. 1

Page 151

7, 14, 21, 28, 35, 42, 49, 56, 63, 70

Page 152

1. 20 ender pearls
2. 30 melons
3. 21 turtle eggs
4. 16 trap doors

Page 153

1. 4 lava blocks
2. 3 honey bottles
3. 8 carrots
4. 5 torches

Page 154

1. 42; 4 tens, 2 ones
2. 64; 6 tens, 4 ones
3. 32; 3 tens, 2 ones
4. 40; 4 tens, 0 ones
5. 30; 3 tens, 0 ones
6. 48; 4 tens, 8 ones
7. 24; 2 tens, 4 ones
8. 21; 2 tens, 1 one

Page 155

1. 10; 1 ten, 0 ones
2. 9; 0 tens, 9 ones
3. 11; 1 ten, 1 one
4. 15; 1 ten, 5 ones
5. 5; 0 tens, 5 ones
6. 14; 1 ten, 4 ones
7. 25; 2 tens, 5 ones
8. 6; 0 tens, 6 ones

Page 156

1. 6
2. 10
3. 14
4. 20
5. 16
6. 18
7. 22
8. 12
9. 24
10. 4
11. 6
12. 16
13. 14
14. 22
15. 10

When you multiply a number by 2, the product is always even.

Page 157

1. 15
2. 40
3. 35
4. 50
5. 45
6. 30
7. 55
8. 20
9. 5
10. 10
11. 15
12. 40
13. 35
14. 55
15. 25

When you multiply an odd number by 5, the product is always odd.

When you multiply an even number by 5, the product is always even.

Page 158

1. 3 hundreds, 4 tens, 2 ones
2. 7 hundreds, 8 tens, 0 ones
3. 9 hundred, 1 tens, 2 ones
4. 8 hundreds, 0 tens, 5 ones
5. 9 hundreds, 2 tens, 6 ones
6. 4 hundreds, 5 tens, 9 ones
7. 6 hundreds, 0 tens, 3 ones
8. 1 hundred, 6 tens, 7 ones

Page 159

8, 16, 24, 32, 40, 48, 56, 64, 72, 80

Page 160

1. 6
2. 5
3. 8
4. 3
5. 4
6. 7
7. 6
8. 9
9. 11

Page 161

A slime

Page 162

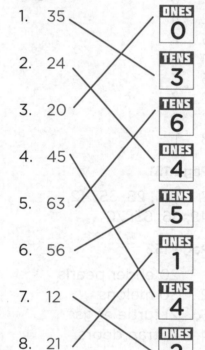

1. 35
2. 24
3. 20
4. 45
5. 63
6. 56
7. 12
8. 21

ONES 0
TENS 3
TENS 6
ONES 4
TENS 5
ONES 1
TENS 4
ONES 2

Page 163

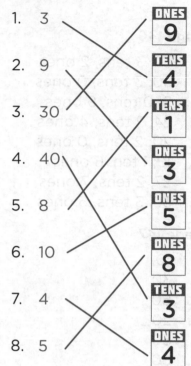

1. 3
2. 9
3. 30
4. 40
5. 8
6. 10
7. 4
8. 5

ONES 9
TENS 4
TENS 1
ONES 3
ONES 5
ONES 8
TENS 3
ONES 4

Page 164

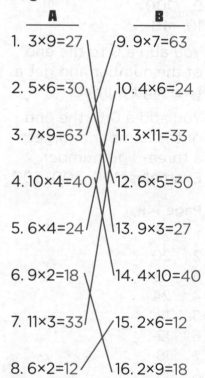

A	B
1. 3×9=27	9. 9×7=63
2. 5×6=30	10. 4×6=24
3. 7×9=63	11. 3×11=33
4. 10×4=40	12. 6×5=30
5. 6×4=24	13. 9×3=27
6. 9×2=18	14. 4×10=40
7. 11×3=33	15. 2×6=12
8. 6×2=12	16. 2×9=18

The order in which you multiply two numbers does not affect the product.

Page 165

1. 12
2. 18
3. 10
4. 24
5. 20
6. 18
7. 27
8. 28

Page 166

1. 36; 40
2. 48; 50
3. 27; 30
4. 12; 10
5. 14; 10
6. 35; 40
7. 20; 20
8. 36; 40
9. 28; 30
10. 20; 20

Page 167

9, 18, 27, 36, 45, 54, 63, 72, 81, 90,

Page 168

1. 35 diamond swords
2. 24 pigs
3. 28 wood blocks
4. 18 TNT blocks

Page 169

1. 5 shelves
2. 10 apples
3. 9 arrows
4. 4 buckets of water

Page 170

1. 300 + 90 + 1
2. 700 + 50 + 6
3. 400 + 00 + 3
4. 100 + 80 + 6
5. 300 + 20 + 9
6. 100 + 60 + 0
7. 400 + 80 + 6
8. 300 + 20 + 9

Page 171

1. 3,000 + 200 + 10 + 4
2. 1,000 + 800 + 40 + 9
3. 6,000 + 700 + 00 + 4
4. 5,000 + 000 + 90 + 6
5. 9,000 + 100 + 30 + 2
6. 4,000 + 800 + 10 + 0
7. 3,000 + 000 + 20 + 1
8. 9,000 + 300 + 00 + 5

Page 172

1. 27
2. 45
3. 63
4. 72
5. 36
6. 9
7. 18
8. 54
9. 36
10. 27
11. 54
12. 9
13. 36
14. 81
15. 18

Page 173

1. 9
2. 6
3. 5
4. 4
5. 8
6. 10
7. 7
8. 3
9. 11
Give it a mirror

Page 174

1. 694
2. 37
3. 201
4. 830
5. 429
6. 504
7. 670
8. 934

Page 175

4, 8, 12, 16, 20, 24, 28, 32, 36, 40

Page 176

1. $63 \div 7 = 9$
2. $24 \div 8 = 3$
3. $36 \div 6 = 6$
4. $20 \div 2 = 10$
5. $54 \div 9 = 6$
6. $35 \div 5 = 7$
7. $24 \div 4 = 6$
8. $27 \div 9 = 3$
9. $25 \div 5 = 5$

Page 177

1. 6 x 3 = 18
2. 7 x 8 = 56
3. 5 x 6 = 30
4. 10 x 4 = 40
5. 5 x 9 = 45
6. 4 x 6 = 24
7. 8 x 8 = 64
8. 10 x 5 = 50
9. 3 x 9 = 27

Page 178

1. 130; 1 hundreds, 3 tens, 0 ones
2. 540; 5 hundreds, 4 tens, 0 ones
3. 430; 4 hundreds, 3 tens, 0 ones
4. 920; 9 hundreds, 2 tens, 0 ones
5. 800; 8 hundreds, 0 tens, 0 ones
6. 340; 3 hundreds, 4 tens, 0 ones
7. 260; 2 hundreds, 6 tens, 0 ones
8. 310; 3 hundreds, 1 ten, 0 ones

It increases by one place value.

Page 179

1. 24; 20
2. 69; 70
3. 43; 40
4. 12; 10
5. 32; 30
6. 47; 50
7. 27; 30
8. 18; 20

Page 180

1. 4
2. 2
3. 1
4. Divide each slice in half
5. Divide each slice into thirds

Page 181

1. 9
2. 28
3. 5
4. 30
5. 7
6. 32
7. 6
8. 27
9. 8

Turn it upside down

Page 182

1. 3,841
2. 4,927
3. 6,041
4. 8,705
5. 342
6. 4,298

Page 183

11, 22, 33, 44, 55, 66, 77, 88, 99, 110

Page 184

2. 30 ÷ 10 = 3
3. 63 ÷ 9 = 7
4. 32 ÷ 4 = 8
5. 28 ÷ 7 = 4
6. 50 ÷ 10 = 5
7. 36 ÷ 6 = 6
8. 20 ÷ 10 = 2
9. 81 ÷ 9 = 9

Page 185

A coat of paint

Page 186

Wording will vary, but the equations should be as follows.

1. 5 x 6 = 30
2. 3 x 6 = 18
3. 6 x 4 = 24

Page 187

Wording will vary, but the equations should be as follows.

1. 28 ÷ 4 = 7
2. 18 ÷ 6 = 3
3. 12 ÷ 4 = 3

Page 188

2. 2 x 8 = 16 swords

3. 4 x 6 = 24 axes

4. 3 x 4 = 12 arrows

5. 5 x 7 = 35 torches

Page 189

2. 30

3. 42

4. 72

5. 56

6. 35

7. 18

8. 48

9. 40

Answer: THE GROUND

Page 190

2. 1,000 + 500 + 0 + 9

3. 8,000 + 0 + 30 + 4

4. 5,000 + 600 + 10 + 2

5. 2,000 + 900 + 10 + 3

6. 7,000 + 300 + 80 + 9

7. 3,000 + 400 + 90 + 0

Page 191

6, 12, 18, 24, 30, 36, 42, 48, 54, 60, 66

Page 192

2. 3:15

3. 12:25

4. 7:40

5. 8:45

6. 2:05

Page 193

1. 14 emeralds

2. 35 emeralds

3. 28 emeralds

4. 42 emeralds

5. The shepherd and the cleric.

6. The fisherman.

7. The tool smith's collection.

Pages 194–195

2. 3 x 5 = 15 fishing rods

3. 3 x 9 = 27 carrots

4. 5 x 7 = 35 pumpkin pies

5. 2 x 6 = 12 elytra

6. 4 x 5 = 20 grass blocks

7. 1 x 7 = 7 shears

8. 4 x 2 = 8 bees

9. 4 x 6 = 24 goats

Hardcore Mode: 4 x 7 = 28 + 6 = 34 skeletons

Pages 196–197

2. 16 diamonds

3. 16 grass blocks

4. 21 buckets of milk

5. 20 eggs

6. 27 wood blocks

7. 15 TNT blocks

8. 7 carrots

9. 18 blocks of snow

Page 198

2. 24, 20

3. 9, 10

4. 49, 50

5. 72, 70

6. 56, 60

7. 30, 30

Page 199

3, 6, 9, 12, 15, 18, 21, 24, 27, 30, 33, 36

Page 200

2. 15 minutes 3. 5 minutes

4. 20 minutes 5. 50 minutes

6. 25 minutes

Page 201

1. 2 nickels

2. 25 pennies

3. 4 nickels

4. 10 dimes

5. 50 pennies

Page 202

1, 3, 5

Creative Mode:

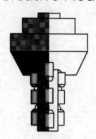

Page 203

1. Area of Alex's wall

   7 x 4 = 28

2. Area of Steve's wall

   5 x 5 = 25

3. Alex's wall

4. 3 more blocks

5. 53

Page 204

1. 3 x 4 = 12

2. 5 x 4 = 20

3. 4 x 4 = 16

4. 2 x 4 = 8

5. 6 x 4 = 24

Page 205

2. 108

3. 96

4. 89

5. 744

6. 32

7. 927

8. 31

9. 372

Answer: NEIGH-BORS

Page 206

2. C

3. F

4. A

5. D

6. G

7. E

Page 207

5, 10, 15, 20, 25, 30, 35, 40, 45, 50, 55, 60

Page 208

2. 3:30

3. 6:05

4. 11:20

5. 8:45

6. 10:10

7. 5:35

8. 12:00

Page 209

1. 115

2. 30

3. 282

4. 180

5. 24

6. 78

7. green

8. pink and black

Hardcore Mode: 709 fish

Pages 210–211

2.

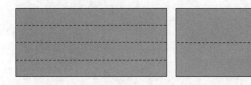

3. Fraction: $\frac{1}{3}$

4. Fraction: $\frac{1}{4}$

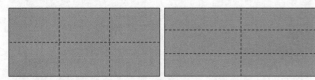

5. Fraction: $\frac{1}{6}$

Page 212

2. 266
3. 432
4. 162
5. 210
6. 392
7. 133
8. 475
Answer: JIFFY CUBE

Page 213

2. 24
3. 10
4. 3
5. 6
6. 9
7. 12
8. 4
9. 11
10. 6

Page 214

1. C
2. A
3. E
4. B
5. D

Page 215

4, 8, 12, 16, 20, 24, 28, 32, 36, 40, 44, 48, 52, 56, 60

Pages 216–217

1. 8, 4
2. 12. 24
3. 25, 40
4. 21, 42

Night Vision Potion: 6, 9, 12, 15
Fermented Spider Eyes: 12, 18, 24, 30

Pages 218–219

1. Current perimeter: 20
New perimeter: 36
2. Current perimeter: 18
New perimeter: 12
3. Current perimeter: 16
New perimeter: 22
4. Current area: 28
New area: 56
5. Current area: 30
New area: 15
6. Current area: 20
New area: 40

Pages 220–221

1. 28 carrots
2. 27 diamonds
3. 24 flowers
4. 5 blocks of iron ore
5. 60 melon pieces
6. 80 arrows
7. 36 bees
8. 18 damage hearts

Page 222

1. 168 (B) 2. 624 (C)
3. 294 (G) 4. 350 (A)
5. 420 (F) 6. 495 (D)
7. 832 (E)

Page 223

1. 180 (F)
2. 103 (D)
3. 228 (A)
4. 738 (B)
5. 336 (G)
6. 294 (C)
7. 91 (E)

Pages 224–225

2. 26 inches
3. 41 inches
4. 44 inches
5. 21 inches

Length in meters	Length in cm	Length in mm
1	100	1,000
3	300	3,000
1.5	150	1,500
2.7	270	2,700
2.3	230	2,300

Pages 226–227

1. obtuse
2. obtuse
3. right
4. obtuse
5. acute
6. right
7. acute
8. obtuse

Page 228

1. 8
2. 120
3. 31
4. 6
5. 28
6. 768
7. 9
8. 85
9. 35

Page 229

1. 156
2. 161
3. 68
4. 78
5. 195
6. 372
Answer: A LIBRARY

Page 230

1. 267, Hundreds: 2
2. 67, Ones: 7
3. 156, Tens: 5
4. 32, Ones: 2
5. 32, Tens: 3
6. 514, Hundreds: 5
7. 58, Ones: 8

Page 231

72, 66, 60, 54, 48, 42, 36, 30, 24, 18, 12, 6

Pages 232–233

1. 13 chickens
2. 39 chickens
3. 23 horses
4. 72 sheep
5. 84 cows
6. 14 cows

	ALEX	STEVE
COWS	14	84
CHICKENS	39	13
SHEEP	72	18
HORSES	23	46

Pages 234–235

1. Bow and arrow: intersecting
2. Experience orb: perpendicular
3. Shears: intersecting
4. Saddle: parallel
5. Tin ingot: parallel
6. Bone: parallel
7. Diamonds: perpendicular

Pages 236–237

1. 50 carrots
2. 13 melon slices
3. 630 books
4. 80 bees
5. 36 enchantments
6. 70 torches
7. 154 slices

Page 238

1. 142, Tens: 4
2. 395, Hundreds: 3
3. 1,945, Thousands: 1
4. 5,472, Ones: 2
5. 37,822, Ten thousands: 3
6. 209, Hundreds: 2
7. 129,908, Hundred thousands: 1

Page 239

20, 40, 80, 160, 320, 640, 1280, 2560, 5120, 10240, 20480, 40960

Page 240

1. $\frac{1}{3}$ is greater, skeleton wins
2. $\frac{3}{4}$ is greater, skeleton wins
3. $\frac{2}{8}$ is greater, ghast wins
4. $\frac{4}{15}$ is greater, skeleton wins
5. $\frac{4}{12}$ is greater, ghast wins
6. $\frac{3}{6}$ is greater, ghast wins
7. $\frac{3}{4}$ is greater, skeleton wins
8. $\frac{4}{6}$ is greater, skeleton wins

Skeleton won the most battles overall.

Page 241

Minutes out of one-fourth day (30 minutes)
Minutes out of half a day (60 minutes)
Minutes out of a day (120 minutes)

$\frac{1}{30}$ $\frac{2}{60}$ $\frac{4}{120}$

$\frac{4}{30}$ $\frac{8}{60}$ $\frac{16}{120}$

$\frac{10}{30}$ $\frac{20}{60}$ $\frac{40}{120}$

$\frac{15}{30}$ $\frac{30}{60}$ $\frac{60}{120}$

Answer: Mining

Pages 242–243

1. 5 feet long
2. 16 bookcases
3. 60 feet wide
4. 192 feet
5. 320 emeralds
6. 10 feet wide
7. 8 feet long

CODE-BREAKING
ACTIVITIES

A PRICKLY SUBJECT

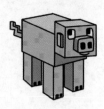

Find the sums of the math problems, then use the code-breaker key to reveal the answer to the joke.

24	25	26	27	28	29	30	31	32	33	34	35	36	37	38
A	B	C	D	E	F	G	H	I	J	K	L	M	N	O

39	40	41	42	43	44	45	46	47	48	49
P	Q	R	S	T	U	V	W	X	Y	Z

What would you get if you could breed a pig with a cactus in the Desert biome?

16 + 8	27 + 12	13 + 25	34 + 7	25 + 9	22 + 26
24					

17 + 25	14 + 25	24 + 8	26 + 11	19 + 9

A _ _ _ _ _ _ _ _ _ _

IN THE BALANCE

Time to rack up some experience!

The first scale is balanced. You must balance the second scale before it tips, lands on the pressure plate, and launches a hidden arrow right at you!

How many 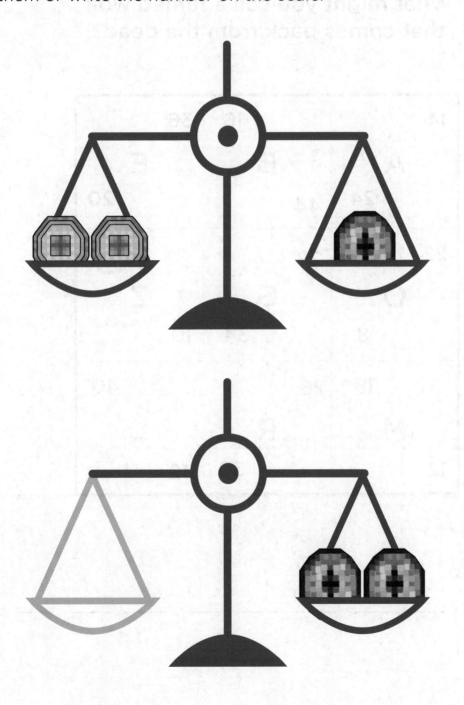 do you need to balance the second scale? Draw them or write the number on the scale.

HILARIOUS HAUNT

Move from box to box as you count by fours. Write the letter from each box where you land on the spaces, in order from left to right. Begin with the number 4 and continue until all the spaces are filled. If you count, hop, and copy letters correctly, you'll reveal the answer to this question:

What might you call a tamed wolf that comes back from the dead?

14 A 24	16 B 44	36 E 20
22 O 8	28 G 34	(4) Z 10
18 M 12	26 R 30	40 L 32

Z _ _ _ _ _ _ _ _

MAGIC NUMBER 1

The numbers at the end of the rows are linked to the images in the grid. What number goes in the circle? This is the magic number for this puzzle.

Circle the problems below that have the magic number as their answer. Unscramble those letters to spell the name of a Minecraft mob.

14 +7	17 −6	4 ×4	7 +9	34 −18
A	T	H	O	L

8 ×2	27 −11	4 ×1	12 +4	25 − 9
N	D	R	P	I

__ __ __ __ __ __ __

A SMASHING SUCCESS

Use the picture-number combination under each blank space to find the correct letter on the grid. The correct letter is the one where the picture and number intersect. If you fill in the spaces correctly, you'll discover a fun tip that can help you be a smashing success!

1	T	K	N	A
2	I	U	H	B
3	G	E	R	M
4	C	W	L	O

A player in a minecart on a rail can ride

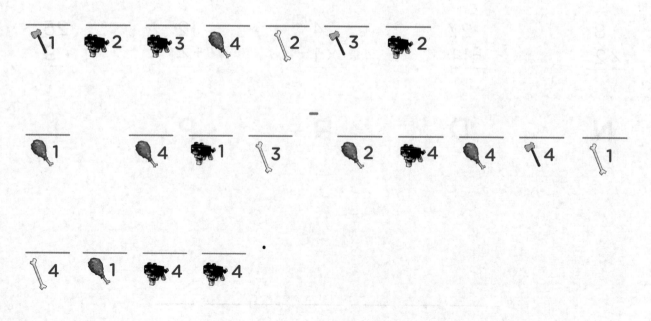

T H R O U G H

A   O N E - B L O C K

W A L L .

TRUTH BE TOLD

Solve this puzzle and unlock a secret before you're attacked by phantoms! Color every box that has an odd number in it to reveal the word that goes in the blank.

Phantoms were going to be _____,

but designers thought they looked like

Nether mobs.

23	35	18	4	7	39	21	32	13	15	26
17	46	11	28	45	40	12	44	35	48	1
5	43	36	20	29	37	50	2	9	14	21
31	24	27	8	41	16	30	22	35	42	37
49	10	25	38	3	33	47	34	29	45	6

TREAT YOURSELF TO THIS TRICK

Solve the math problems, then use the code-breaker key to treat yourself to a trick you can play on your Minecrafting friends.

32	33	34	35	36	37	38	39	40	41	42	43	44	45	46
A	B	C	D	E	F	G	H	I	J	K	L	M	N	O

47	48	49	50	51	52	53	54	55	56	57
P	Q	R	S	T	U	V	W	X	Y	Z

Do this with ice blocks, slime, or soul sand:

$$63 - 24 = \boxed{}$$
$$53 - 13 = \boxed{}$$
$$99 - 64 = \boxed{}$$
$$88 - 52 = \boxed{}$$
$$69 - 29 = \boxed{}$$
$$89 - 38 = \boxed{}$$

$$81 - 29 = \boxed{}$$
$$62 - 17 = \boxed{}$$
$$76 - 41 = \boxed{}$$
$$63 - 27 = \boxed{}$$
$$91 - 42 = \boxed{}$$

$$92 - 58 = \boxed{}$$
$$78 - 46 = \boxed{}$$
$$65 - 16 = \boxed{}$$
$$54 - 7 = \boxed{}$$
$$47 - 11 = \boxed{}$$
$$90 - 39 = \boxed{}$$

__ __ __ __ __ __

__ __ __ __ __ __ __ __ __ __ __ __

DON'T LET IT ROLL

The first scale is balanced. The second scale is not, and those spawn eggs are about to roll and start a dangerous chain reaction! How many do you need to balance the second scale? Draw them or write the number on the scale.

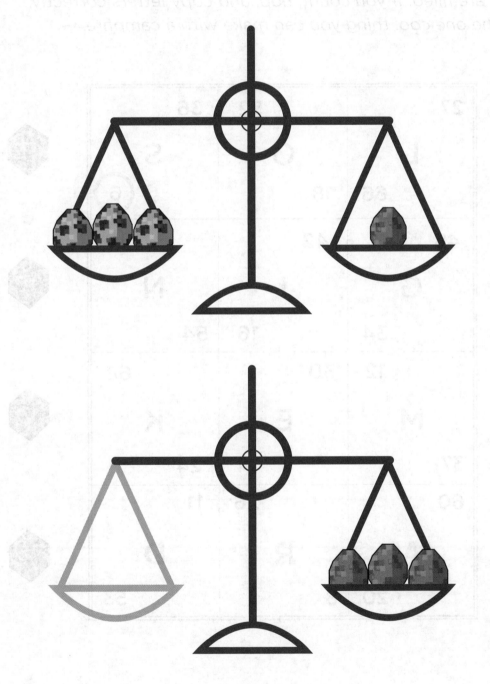

FIRE AWAY

Campfires are useful. Do you know why?

Move from box to box as you count by sixes. Write the letter from each box where you land on the spaces, in order from left to right. Begin with the number 6 and continue until all the spaces are filled. If you count, hop, and copy letters correctly, you'll reveal the one cool thing you can make with a campfire.

27		52	36
L		O	S
66	18		6
48		42	10
G		I	N
34		16	54
12	30		68
M	E		K
37		14	24
60		26	11
A		R	D
20	8		53

S _ _ _ _   _ _ _ _ _ _

MAGIC NUMBER II

Have you ever seen this mob spawn naturally?

The numbers at the end of the rows and columns are linked to the images in the grid. What number goes in the circle? This is the magic number for this puzzle.

			20
			24
			◯
29	18	25	

Circle problems below that have the magic number as their answer. Unscramble those letters to spell the name of the Minecraft mob that has a very rare 0.164% chance of spawning naturally.

37 − 9	2 ×14	22 +14	16 +12	21 + 7	84 ÷ 3
I	E	O	H	E	N

41 − 13	35 − 7	56 ÷ 3	17 +11	4 ×7
S	P	N	K	P

__ __ __ __   __ __ __ __ __

HERE, BOY

Use the picture-number combination under each missing letter space to find the correct letter on the grid. The correct letter is the one where the picture and number intersect. If you fill in the spaces correctly, you'll discover the answer to the riddle.

Why are illusioners like well-trained dogs?

	🐐	🐟	🦜	🧟
1	G	P	A	S
2	O	F	H	C
3	D	I	E	Z
4	L	M	N	R

They come on

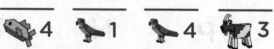

___ ___ ___ ___ ___ ___ ___
2   2   4   4   1   4   3

"WE ARE NUMBER 2, HEY!"

Hidden in the grid is a mixed-up mob. It's cheering about being #2. Color every box that has an even number in it, then unscramble the letters to reveal a second-place mob and write it on the line.

74	16	32	49	2	43	98	69	43	80	67	89	28	76	10	58	65	96	38	62
59	4	85	97	90	25	6	37	74	77	26	17	50	51	33	81	9	44	91	19
39	28	73	39	34	16	22	77	62	26	18	99	32	47	6	88	67	6	18	52
75	86	7	55	68	27	38	63	8	93	30	45	16	55	79	74	29	23	11	68
41	54	57	95	72	3	56	25	86	61	44	83	66	84	38	22	35	24	76	94

Unscrambled letters:

— — — — —

Do you know in what way this mob comes in second?

_____

267

STEVE SAYS

Steve has a Minecraft saying that he thinks is super clever. Solve the math problems, then use the code-breaker key to complete Steve's favorite saying.

21	22	23	24	25	26	27	28	29	30	31	32	33	34	35
A	B	C	D	E	F	G	H	I	J	K	L	M	N	O

36	37	38	39	40	41	42	43	44	45	46
P	Q	R	S	T	U	V	W	X	Y	Z

Steve's favorite saying:

3 × 9	5 × 5	5 × 7	8 × 4	7 × 5	1 × 27	15 × 3
27						

G __ __ __ __ __ __

rocks, but

3 × 9	25 × 1	7 × 5	27 × 1	19 × 2	3 × 7	6 × 6	4 × 7	9 × 5

__ __ __ __ __ __ __ __ __

is where it's at!

ENDLESS ENCHANTMENTS

The first and second scales are balanced. How many 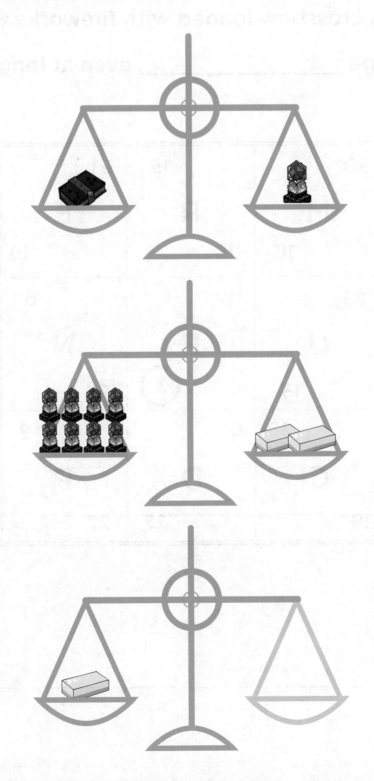 do you need to balance the third scale? Draw them or write the number on the scale. If you balance the scale correctly, you will be able to enchant every item in your inventory!

FIRE POWER

Move from box to box as you count by threes. Write the letter from each box where you land on the spaces, in order from left to right. Begin with the number 3 and continue until all the spaces are filled. If you count, hop, and copy letters correctly, you'll fill in the blank below.

A crossbow loaded with fireworks will

damage _____, even at long range.

30 M 18	15 R 25	21 E 19
23 U 13	12 E (3)	6 N 24
28 C 16	9 D 27	8 P 22

E _ _ _ _ _ _ _

MAGIC NUMBER III

If you fail to solve this puzzle, your ship is sunk!

The numbers at the end of the rows and columns are linked to the images in the grid. What number goes in the circle? This is the magic number for this puzzle.

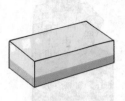

			41
			31
			27
33	◯	31	

Circle the problems below that have the magic number as their answer. Unscramble those letters to spell the answer to the joke.

Why did the Nitwit sink the boat with too much iron, gold, and redstone?

19 +16	5 ×7	4 ×8	47 −12	57 −22	49 − 7
E	N	J	O	S	G

28 + 7	32 + 3	41 − 6	6 ×2	7 ×5	21 +14
D	A	E	K	I	R

Because he heard the captain say,

"   "

___ ___ ___ ___ ___   ___ ___ ___ ___.

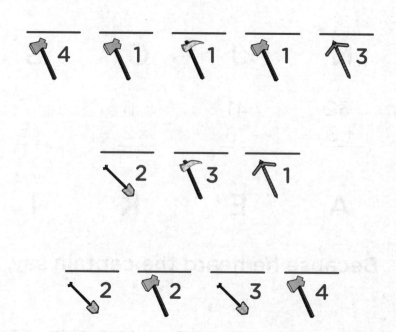

SPUH-LASH

Splash texts are the yellow lines of text on the title screen. They might be inside jokes, bits of advice, or nonsense.

Use the picture-number combination under each missing letter space to find the correct letter on the grid. The correct letter is the one where the picture and number intersect. If you fill in the spaces correctly, you'll discover splash text that's also a useful piece of Minecraft advice.

1	G	V	E	U
2	A	P	O	D
3	R	I	H	W
4	Z	C	N	T

HUNT AND FIND

Color every box that has a multiple of 2 in it to discover what's hidden in the grid. There's loot in it for you, if you can find it.

24	86	12	10	58
68	51	17	25	44
1	70	94	36	73
23	81	35	47	13
26	82	54	18	4
48	95	41	5	33
62	22	34	72	20
9	69	15	21	51
16	40	6	76	94
11	37	19	28	7
31	43	82	61	53
36	50	66	18	70
55	3	45	21	59
2	88	46	72	98
54	25	79	19	26
90	71	94	89	38
38	42	6	83	14
57	93	59	37	53
64	10	78	94	26
54	75	62	29	72
26	39	85	1	34
13	27	65	61	11
74	16	28	50	74
68	39	15	97	92
24	52	60	78	30
87	31	23	99	67
18	34	62	90	58
43	9	55	22	41
17	35	30	57	3
96	68	42	56	74

What? You can't read it? Try turning the page on its side.

INSIDE RIDDLE

The letters in the code-breaker key spell the answers to both riddles below. Solve the math problems to decipher the answer to the first riddle. Then cross off those letters inside the code-breaker key to reveal the answer to the second riddle.

What large object sometimes generates on a beach?

13	14	15	16	17	18	19	20	21	22	23	24	25	26	27	28
I	S	H	C	I	E	P	W	B	R	E	E	R	C	K	G

$$12 + 2 = 14 \quad 31 - 16 = \square \quad 6 + 11 = \square \quad 27 - 8 = \square \quad 5 \times 4 = \square \quad 17 + 5 = \square \quad 6 \times 4 = \square \quad 34 - 8 = \square \quad 9 \times 3 = \square$$

S _ _ _ _ _ _ _ _

Where else does it generate?

_ _ _ _ _ _ _

UNDER PRESSURE

The first and second scales are balanced. How many 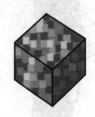 do you need to balance the third scale? Draw them or write the number on the scale.

If you balance the scale correctly, you'll keep the blocks from rolling off the scale and avoid a dangerous chain reaction.

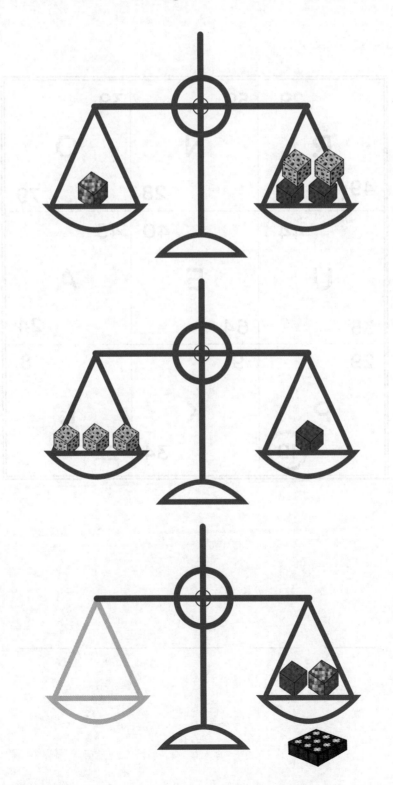

JUMP FIVE

Beginning with the number 19, jump from box to box by adding 5 each time you move. Write the letter from each box where you land on the blank letter spaces, in order from left to right. You'll reveal a Minecraft game where players jump around.

29 R 49	59 N 28	39 O 79
44 U 35	40 E 64	45 A 24
29 P (19)	9 K 34	8 L 22

P __ __ __ __ __ __

MAGIC NUMBER IV

The numbers at the end of the rows are linked to the images in the grid. What number goes in the circle? This is the magic number.

mooshroom	mooshroom	horse	skeleton	**35**
skeleton	mooshroom	skeleton	horse	◯
skeleton	skeleton	horse	horse	**22**
horse	horse	horse	horse	**16**

Circle the problems below that have the magic number as their answer. Unscramble those letters to spell the name of a Minecraft mob.

28 +2	6 ×5	26 +4	33 −22	17 +24	15 ×2
N	L	G	I	R	E

21 +9	51 −11	16 +14	76 −46	53 −23	42 −12
W	C	O	M	S	O

___ ___ ___ ___   ___ ___ ___ ___ ___

SLOW GOING

Cobwebs are great for slowing down mobs and arrows, but they have another clever use, too.

Use the picture-number combination under each blank letter space to find the correct letter on the grid. The correct letter is the one where the picture and number intersect. If you fill in the spaces correctly, you'll discover another fun use for cobwebs.

Use cobwebs to create delays in _____.

1	D	A	T	N
2	U	B	K	R
3	O	C	S	G
4	W	E	L	I

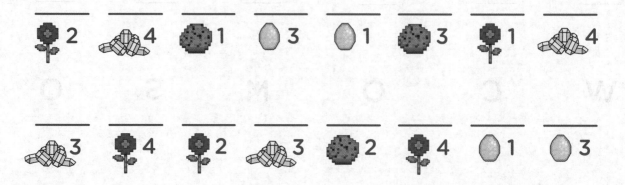

A SPILLED SECRET

It's more of a cure than a secret, really, but you still don't want to spill it.

Color every box that has a multiple of 3 in it to reveal this handy item.

78	84	22	30	18	65	6	16	75	49	69	20	53	99
36	17	60	43	45	70	41	35	90	4	33	64	42	58
57	14	51	65	24	88	42	50	27	31	51	96	56	44
21	2	28	91	33	61	54	11	63	73	45	62	39	27
45	37	19	8	42	7	15	26	48	56	60	7	22	75

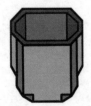
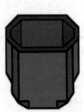
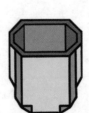

ALERT! ALERT! ALERT!

Use this handy trick to stay safe when you're working in your Minecraft house . . . or office . . . or lab . . . or anywhere indoors.

Solve the math problems, then use the code-breaker key to reveal this useful tip.

14	15	16	17	18	19	20	21	22	23	24	25	26	27	28
A	B	C	D	E	F	G	H	I	J	K	L	M	N	O

29	30	31	32	33	34	35	36	37	38	39
P	Q	R	S	T	U	V	W	X	Y	Z

If you want to hear when hostile mobs are approaching, surround your building with

18 + 11	5 × 5	22 − 8	54 ÷ 2	3 × 8	28 + 4
29					

P __ __ __ __ __ .

A BALANCED DIET

You've gotta eat to survive!

The first and second scales are balanced. How many 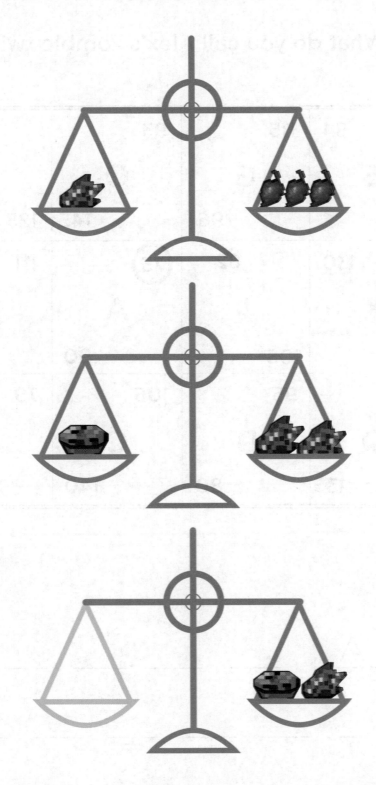 do you need to balance the third scale? Draw them or write the number on the scale.

If you balance the scale correctly, you will refill your hunger bar.

TWINZIES

Beginning with the number 75, count up by fives. Write the letter from each box where you land on the spaces, in order from left to right until all spaces are filled.

If you count, hop, and copy letters correctly, you'll reveal the answer to this question:

What do you call Alex's zombie twin?

84	115	93	100
E	G	O	R
120	96	145 125	
130	82	(75)	111
X	I	A	E
99	105	90	85
101	95	106	79
O	D	C	N
135	80	140	110

A __ __ __ __

__ __ __ __ __ __

MAGIC NUMBER V

The numbers at the end of the rows are linked to the images in the grid. What number goes in the circle? This is the magic number for this puzzle.

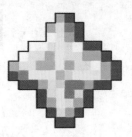

🐖	🐖	🐕	⛏	**61**
⛏	🐖	⛏	🐕	◯
⛏	⛏	🐕	🐕	**70**
🐕	🐕	🐕	🐕	**80**

Circle the problems below that have the magic number as their answer. Unscramble those letters to reveal a play mode that gives you more control over the Minecraft world.

76 −13	8 ×7	45 + 2	7 ×9	91 −28
F	N	A	U	F

98 −34	47 +16	84 −19	21 x 3	28 +35
G	B	B	E	T

— — — — —

LOOKING UP

Have you ever gotten lost in Minecraft? Use the picture-number combination under each blank letter space to find the correct letter on the grid. The correct letter is the one where the picture and number intersect. If you fill in the spaces correctly, you'll discover a unique method for finding your way in Minecraft.

	<cloud>	<block>	<sun>	<arrows>
1	O	A	T	H
2	Y	P	E	M
3	B	K	W	R
4	L	V	X	S

Watch the sun, moon, stars, and clouds, because they

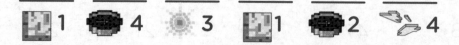

GET SOME PERSPECTIVE

Color every box that has a multiple of 5 to reveal the key on your keyboard that changes your view in the game from first person to third person. Hint: *The answer lies in the uncolored squares.*

What is the key? _____

14	58	22	30	17	63	92
39	75	15	50	87	20	45
66	4	60	25	51	42	6
48	80	5	40	35	10	27
52	65	70	55	11	49	88

WHAT IS THE MEANING OF THIS?

Solve the math problems, then use the code-breaker key to reveal a fun fact about the company that makes Minecraft.

48	49	50	51	52	53	54	55	56	57	58	59	60	61	62
A	B	C	D	E	F	G	H	I	J	K	L	M	N	O

63	64	65	66	67	68	69	70	71	72	73
P	Q	R	S	T	U	V	W	X	Y	Z

$$20 \times 3 \qquad 38 + 24 \qquad 19 \times 3 \qquad 96 \div 2 \qquad 98 - 37 \qquad 18 \times 3$$

" 60 ☐ ☐ ☐ ☐ ☐ "   is a

M _ _ _ _ _

$$99 - 33 \quad 35 \times 2 \quad 43 + 9 \quad 17 \times 3 \quad 72 - 16 \quad 38 + 28 \quad 11 \times 5 \qquad 10 \times 7 \quad 18 + 44 \quad 84 - 19 \quad 93 - 42$$

☐ ☐ ☐ ☐ ☐ ☐ ☐   ☐ ☐ ☐ ☐

_ _ _ _ _ _ _   _ _ _ _

$$9 \times 6 \qquad 29 + 19 \qquad 73 - 22 \qquad 48 + 6 \qquad 71 - 19 \qquad 33 + 34$$

meaning " ☐ ☐ ☐ ☐ ☐ ☐ " .

_ _ _ _ _ _

PAYMENT BALANCE

Villagers insist you balance the payment scales below. If you don't, they vow to pillage your inventory.

The first and second scales are balanced. How many 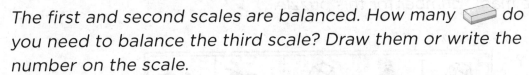 do you need to balance the third scale? Draw them or write the number on the scale.

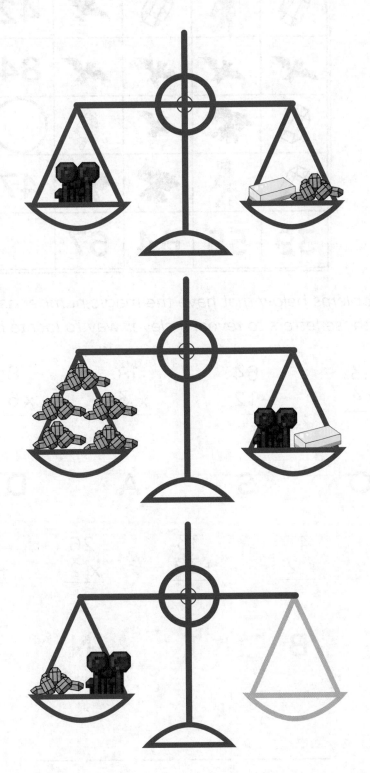

MAGIC NUMBER VI

The numbers at the end of the rows and columns are linked to the images in the grid. What number goes in the circle? This is the magic number for this puzzle.

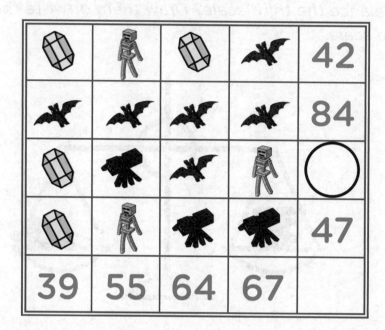

Circle the problems below that have the magic number as their answer. Unscramble those letters to reveal a clever way to locate hidden caves.

79	13	64	18	8	25
−25	×4	−12	× 3	×6	+27

E   O   S   A   D   P

78	41	13	26	80
−26	+ 2	+39	× 2	+24

I   B   T   N   C

___ ___ ___ ___ ___ ___

PRO BUILDER TIP

Design and build cool structures and scenes with this pro tip.

Use the picture-number combination under each blank letter space to find the correct letter on the grid. The correct letter is the one where the picture and number intersect. If you fill in the spaces correctly, you'll discover a unique method for crafting amazing buildings and landscapes.

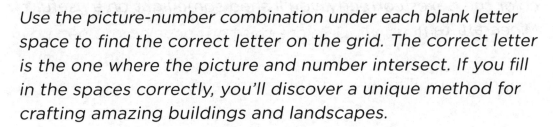

	●	▦	▨	⛏
1	I	T	L	R
2	W	E	U	A
3	N	Q	S	H
4	M	G	V	D

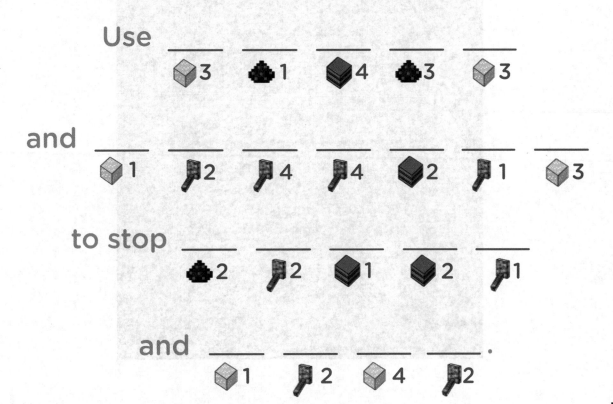

Use ⬜3 ●1 ▦4 ●3 ⬜3

and ⬜1 ⛏2 ⛏4 ⛏4 ▦2 ⛏1 ⬜3

to stop ●2 ⛏2 ▦1 ▦2 ⛏1

and ⬜1 ⛏2 ⬜4 ⛏2 .

HIDDEN RESOURCE

Color every box with a number that is divisible by 3. If you color the boxes correctly, you'll shed some light on a useful Minecraft item.

33	15	81	86	75	39	24	70	66	30	72	11	72	3	18	34	75	19	87
8	90	76	35	42	89	51	43	93	91	87	82	36	55	96	74	99	61	57
26	48	41	20	96	14	78	1	6	12	54	2	21	59	79	25	15	60	24
77	63	67	47	36	83	45	88	54	81	32	65	9	17	42	68	51	80	39
49	9	22	40	21	69	18	71	84	94	90	85	48	66	84	46	78	13	45

Is there such a thing as too many Minecraft jokes? Neigh!

Find the sums of the math problems, then use the code-breaker key to decipher the punchline of this joke.

48	49	50	51	52	53	54	55	56	57	58	59	60	61	62
A	B	C	D	E	F	G	H	I	J	K	L	M	N	O

63	64	65	66	67	68	69	70	71	72	73
P	Q	R	S	T	U	V	W	X	Y	Z

Alex calls her horse "Mayo," and

54 +12	27 +35	69 − 9	31 +21	12 +55	63 − 7	34 + 26	11 +41	22 x 3
66								
S	___	___	___	___	___	___	___	___

31 +29	64 − 16	31 +41	31 x 2	90 − 29	75 − 23	8 X 7	84 − 30	72 − 17	11 X 6
___	___	___	___	___	___	___	___	___	___

THE POINT IS... SHARP!

The first and second scales are balanced. How many  do you need to balance the third scale? Draw them or write the number on the scale before the cactus rolls and you feel its spikes. Ouch!

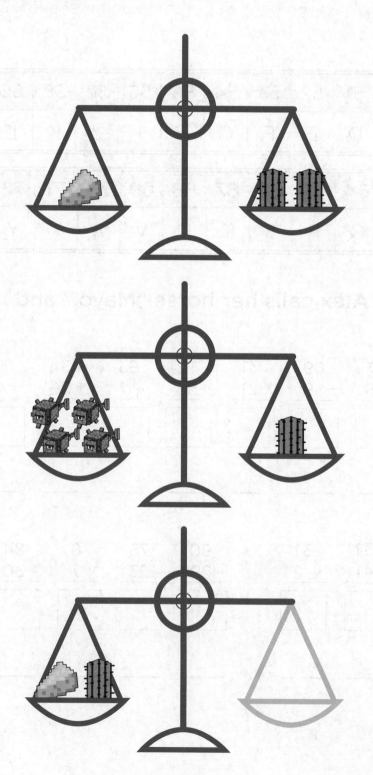

ASK AND RECEIVE

Hop from box to box counting by sevens. Write the letter from each box where you land on the spaces, in order from left to right, until all spaces are filled.

If you count, hop, and copy letters correctly, you'll reveal the decorative item that was added at the suggestion of a Minecraft fan like you.

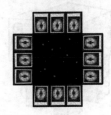

31 I ⑦	35 F 46	62 U 45	56 M 28
60 R 42	70 S 25	22 T 14	38 Y 29
50 D 13	24 Q 32	63 E 21	43 A 49

I _ _ _ _

_ _ _ _ _ _

293

MAGIC NUMBER VII

The numbers at the end of the rows and columns are linked to the images in the grid. What number goes in the circle? This is the magic number for this puzzle.

				43
				53
				42
				53
◯	52	40	51	

Circle the problems below that have the magic number as their answer. Unscramble those letters to spell the name of a Minecraft mob.

6 × 8	17 +31	2 × 24	57 − 9	7 × 7	36 +13
S	I	H	L	A	B

60 −12	12 × 4	33 +15	4 × 12	16 × 3	29 +19
R	S	V	F	E	I

_ _ _ _ _ _ _

ZOMBIE-PROOF

Use the picture-number combination under each space to find the correct letter on the grid. The correct letter is the one where the picture and number intersect. If you fill in the spaces correctly, you'll discover a useful Minecraft tip for protecting yourself from zombies.

	![]	![]	![]	![]
1	O	V	C	I
2	B	S	L	D
3	F	G	R	M
4	J	N	A	E

Want to zombie-proof your castle?

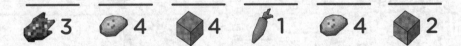

$\underline{\hphantom{F}}_{3}\ \underline{\hphantom{F}}_{4}\ \underline{\hphantom{F}}_{4}\ \underline{\hphantom{F}}_{1}\ \underline{\hphantom{F}}_{4}\ \underline{\hphantom{F}}_{2}$

make excellent

$\underline{\hphantom{F}}_{2}\ \underline{\hphantom{F}}_{1}\ \underline{\hphantom{F}}_{1}\ \underline{\hphantom{F}}_{3}\ \underline{\hphantom{F}}_{2}$

A MINECRAFT CHALLENGE

Solve this puzzle to reveal a particular kind of Minecraft challenge! Color every box with a number that is divisible by 4.

92	32	60	14	96	12	68	58	8	38	22	54	96
56	34	4	22	78	44	18	70	64	28	10	24	48
24	62	14	30	38	84	42	46	88	72	36	56	52
80	94	48	74	66	52	10	82	40	98	92	26	16
36	72	16	50	18	20	34	26	76	90	86	42	68

HIDDEN PASSAGE

Use your math skills to crack the code. Solve the math problems and use the code-breaker key to find the letters that spell out where you can find a hidden passage.

9	10	11	12	13	14	15	16	17	18
S	E	T	N	R	D	O	P	N	O

19	20	21	22	23	24	25	26	27
G	R	H	T	O	A	L	L	D

$$3 \times 3 \qquad 45 - 34 \qquad 7 + 6 \qquad 24 - 9 \qquad 15 + 2 \qquad 12 + 7 \qquad 3 \times 7 \qquad 31 - 8 \qquad 5 \times 5 \qquad 19 + 8$$

☐ ☐ ☐ ☐ ☐ ☐ ☐ ☐ ☐ ☐

Now, cross out the letters you used in the code-breaker key and write the remaining letters in order on the space below.

What is the hidden passage called?

_____

YOUR FATE, IN THE BALANCE

As long as the scales are balanced, you are safe. As soon as one tips, even the slightest bit, you're a goner. The first and second scales are balanced. How many  do you need to balance the third scale? Draw them or write the number on the scale before the lava or the husks destroy you!

A NETHER JOKE

Beginning with the number 14, move from box to box by adding 3 each time you move. Write the letter from each box where you land on the spaces, in order from left to right, until all spaces are filled. If you count, hop, and copy letters correctly, you'll reveal the punchline to this joke:

Did you hear about the Minecraft player who went to sleep in the Nether?

20 C	50 E 29	23 A 38	53 N 46
11			
35 O	14 H 55	22 A 33	32 T 51
59			
26 M	47 D	17 E	8 B
37	56	44	41

H __ __   __ __ __ __ __   __ __   __   __ __ __

__ __ __   __ __ __   __ __ !

299

MAGIC NUMBER VIII

The numbers at the end of the rows and columns are linked to the images in the grid. What number goes in the circle? This is the magic number for this puzzle.

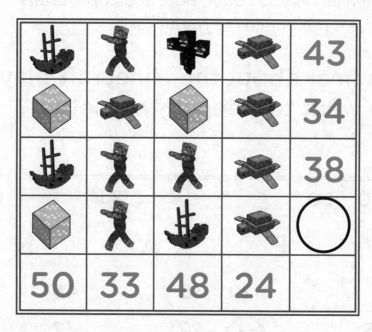

				43
				34
				38
				◯
50	33	48	24	

Circle the problems below that have the magic number as their answer. Unscramble those letters to spell the name of a new, underwater block that can be activated to attack hostile mobs.

8 x 5	18 +13	26 +14	48 – 8	4 x 10
D	E	I	U	C

57 –17	2 x20	47 – 9	62 x 2	27 +13
N	T	L	S	O

___ ___ ___ ___ ___ ___

AIM HIGH

Reaching higher altitudes is possible only if you know this trick. Use the picture-number combination under each blank letter space to find the correct letter on the grid. The correct letter is the one where the picture and number intersect. If you fill in the spaces correctly, you'll discover a useful Minecraft skill.

	🦜	🛤	➡	🐉
1	L	N	E	J
2	C	U	P	G
3	I	S	T	R
4	O	A	M	K

____ ____ ____ ____ ____ ____
➡2 🦜3 🦜1 🦜1 🛤4 🐉3

____ ____ ____ ____ ____ ____ ____
🐉1 🛤2 ➡4 ➡2 🦜3 🛤1 🐉2

MINECRAFT LINGO

Are you up on Minecraft lingo? Color every box that contains a multiple of 7. If you color the boxes correctly, you'll reveal a term that competitive Minecrafters know.

37	54	77	47	38	84	32	94	60	81	42
64	50	35	92	28	61	14	37	45	34	91
70	14	63	59	56	43	77	65	98	42	56
84	73	7	31	42	72	63	52	35	86	49
98	21	49	87	91	36	14	46	70	28	7

Wait a minute, that's not right! Try turning the book upside down to read the term for competitive gaming.

A DIFFERENT POV

Solve the math problems, then use the code-breaker key to figure out which option in Minecraft allows you to turn everything black and white or upside down.

37	38	39	40	41	42	43	44	45	46	47	48	49	50	51
A	B	C	D	E	F	G	H	I	J	K	L	M	N	O

52	53	54	55	56	57	58	59	60	61	62
P	Q	R	S	T	U	V	W	X	Y	Z

14	19	13	39	70
+ 41	x 3	x 4	+ 2	– 16
55				

S   __   __   __   __

81	66	40	42	26	14
– 26	– 25	– 1	+12	+15	x 4

__   __   __   __   __   __

37	80	67	48	9	77	27	72
+18	– 39	– 11	+ 8	x 5	– 27	+16	– 17

__   __   __   __   __   __   __   __

A SLIMING SCALE

The first and second scales are balanced. How many  do you need to balance the third scale? Draw them or write the number on the scale. If you balance the scale correctly, you get to keep the redstone.

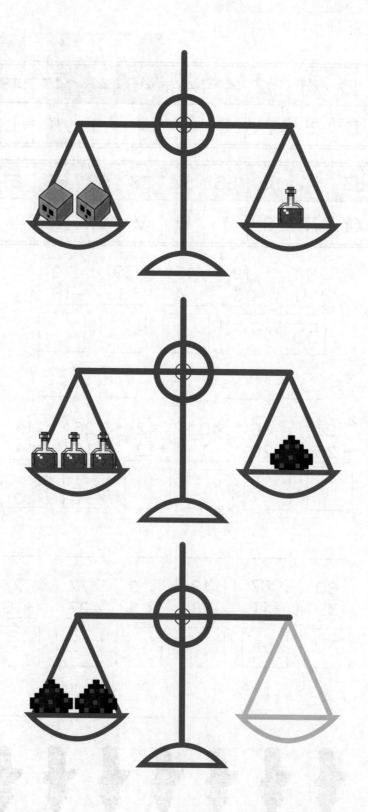

MINING SHORTCUT

This shortcut can save you tons of time. Beginning with the number 22, move from box to box by adding 4 each time you move. Write the letter from each box where you land on the spaces, in order from left to right, until all spaces are filled. If you count, hop, and copy letters correctly, you'll reveal a time-saving mining technique.

30 86		78	82
N	S	H	E
84	(22)	56	54
25	58 42		34
I	L	R	D
72	32	70	40
66	92	52	88
O	G	Y	T
90	38	60	62
50 80		46	74
V	F	A	C
94	76 26		64

Mine S _N_ _D_ _D_ and _G_ _R_ _A_ _V_ _E_ _L_

with _T_ _O_ _R_ _C_ _H_ _E_ _S_ .

FALL FIX

Have you ever been destroyed in the game by a bad fall? Next time, use this to survive. Solve the math problems, then use the code-breaker key to reveal a handy tip for avoiding falls.

45	46	47	48	49	50	51	52	53	54	55	56	57	58	59
A	B	C	D	E	F	G	H	I	J	K	L	M	N	O

60	61	62	63	64	65	66	67	68	69	70
P	Q	R	S	T	U	V	W	X	Y	Z

$$\begin{array}{c} 15 \\ \times\ 3 \\ \hline \boxed{45} \end{array} \qquad \begin{array}{c} 61 \\ -\ 15 \\ \hline \ \end{array} \qquad \begin{array}{c} 5 \\ \times\ 13 \\ \hline \ \end{array} \qquad \begin{array}{c} 38 \\ +\ 9 \\ \hline \ \end{array} \qquad \begin{array}{c} 98 \\ -\ 43 \\ \hline \ \end{array} \qquad \begin{array}{c} 7 \\ \times\ 7 \\ \hline \ \end{array} \qquad \begin{array}{c} 8 \\ \times\ 8 \\ \hline \ \end{array}$$

A __ __ __ __ __ __

$$\begin{array}{c} 32 \\ +\ 27 \\ \hline \ \end{array} \qquad \begin{array}{c} 10 \\ \times\ 5 \\ \hline \ \end{array} \qquad \begin{array}{c} 91 \\ -\ 24 \\ \hline \ \end{array} \qquad \begin{array}{c} 43 \\ +\ 2 \\ \hline \ \end{array} \qquad \begin{array}{c} 16 \\ \times\ 4 \\ \hline \ \end{array} \qquad \begin{array}{c} 82 \\ -\ 33 \\ \hline \ \end{array} \qquad \begin{array}{c} 27 \\ +\ 35 \\ \hline \ \end{array}$$

__ __ __ __ __ __ __

BALANCE OF NATURE

Can you preserve the delicate balance of nature? The first and second scales are balanced. How many 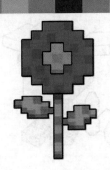 do you need to balance the third scale? Draw them or write the number on the scale.

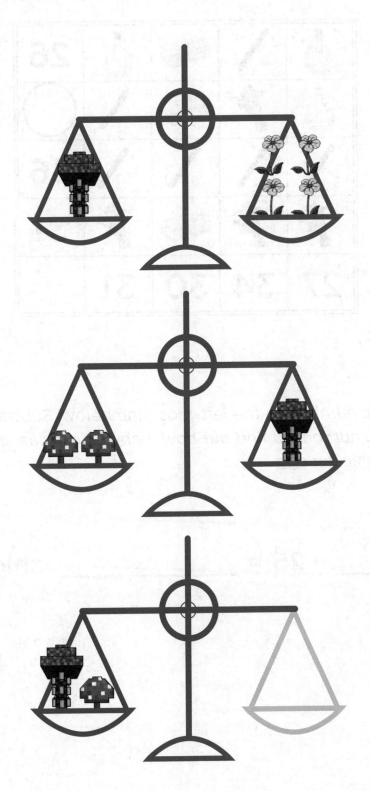

MAGIC NUMBER IX

The numbers at the end of the rows and columns are linked to the images in the grid. What number goes in the circle? This is the magic number for this puzzle.

Write the magic number on the left-most line below. Subtract 25 from this magic number to find out how many chicks can spawn from one Minecraft chicken egg.

_____ – 25 = _____ chicks

ANSWER KEY

PAGE 256

A PORKYSPINE

PAGE 257

4 experience orbs

PAGE 258

ZOMBEAGLE

PAGE 259

16 - DOLPHIN

PAGE 260

A player in a minecart on a rail can ride THROUGH A ONE-BLOCK WALL

PAGE 261

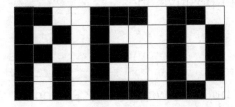

PAGE 262

Do this with ice blocks, slime, or soul sand: HIDE IT UNDER CARPET. Friends won't see it, but the effects will still work, so they'll slip, bounce, or slooooooow down.

PAGE 263

9 zombie pigman spawn eggs

PAGE 264

SMOKE SIGNAL

PAGE 265

28 - PINK SHEEP

PAGE 266

They come on COMMAND.
Get it? Illusioners don't spawn naturally, but you can make them spawn with the /summon illusioner command.

PAGE 267

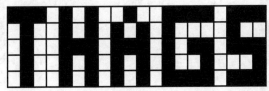

The mob is the GHAST, and it is the second largest mob in Minecraft. The Ender Dragon is largest.

PAGE 268

GEOLOGY rocks, but GEOGRAPHY is where it's at!

PAGE 269

4 enchanted books

PAGE 270

ENDERMEN

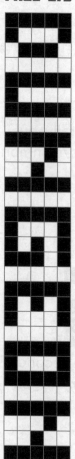

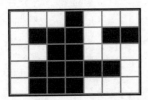

PAGE 295

FENCES make excellent DOORS. Zombies can't break the fences, and you can fight back through the fences. Genius!

PAGE 296

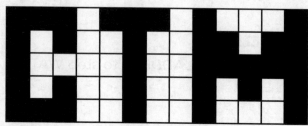

CTM (Complete the Monument.)

PAGE 297

STRONGHOLD
END PORTAL

PAGE 298

9 evokers

PAGE 299

Did you hear about the Minecraft player who went to sleep in the Nether? HE CAME TO A BED END.

PAGE 300

40 - CONDUIT

PAGE 301

PILLAR JUMPING - The pillar is placed while you're jumping.

PAGE 302

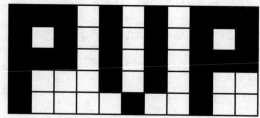

PVP stands for Player vs. Player.

PAGE 303

SUPER SECRET SETTINGS

PAGE 304

12 slime blocks

PAGE 305

Mine SAND and GRAVEL with TORCHES.

PAGE 306

A BUCKET OF WATER

PAGE 307

6 flowers

PAGE 308

29 - 4 chicks